The Life I Want in Christ

by

Michael Frank Sabo

Foreword by Ted Ward

The Life I Want in Christ

Bibliographic Citation

Sabo, Michael Frank. 2012. *The Life I Want in Christ*. 3rd edition.

Printed in the United States of America
First printing 2012

Original Cover by Thomas Hirschler
Original Design and Layout by Grant Hoekstra and Wayne Kijanowski
Original Style and Format by Melody Hirschler
Original Edit by Stacey L. Douglas
3rd Edition by Mark Simpson

Credits

To my dad and mom,
Frank and Laura Sabo

Apart from my salvation,
you have been the greatest expression
of God's grace to me

§§§

In Memoriam
Larry S. Ebert

Contents

Acknowledgments

Certainly the seeds for this book and its actual writing and editing were a community effort. Thanks are expressed to Dr. Ted Ward for his guidance and friendship through the years. His insights on the educational implications of Scripture have had a profound effect upon my life and this book. I am also indebted to Dr. Robert Coleman for his godly example. Through our times of prayer and personal interaction I have been deeply drawn to our heavenly Father.

The honest and critical feedback from numerous individuals have made this book more relevant and readable to a larger community. To them I say thank you and acknowledge that they too have had a valuable part in the production of this book. These individuals are Rick Albertson, Tim Bhajjan, Jim Brisson Jr., Brian Cain, Candice Cardinale, Bill Cargill, Robert Coleman, David English, Carol Forsythe, Jane Goleman, Bill Graddy, Thomas Hirschler, F.B. Huey, Bob Lewis, Grant Osborne, Brett Reider, and Ted Ward. Thanks to Grant Hoekstra and Wayne Kijanowski for their expertise related to formatting and graphics. Gratitude to Stacey L. Douglas and his friend John Dichtl for the book's title and to Thomas and Melody Hirschler for the book's cover design and editing of style and format. Special thanks to Stacey for his encouragement, insight, and skillful editing which has enabled this book to become more readable and to reach a broader audience.

The greatest expression of gratitude is extended to my wife, Darlene, who has helped me express the truths of this book not only in my writing but more importantly, in my life!

Foreword by Ted Ward

Nothing is more important to effective evangelizing than the Christian's own walk with Christ. Today's skeptical world has seen too much of the hollowness of claims about Christ that are denied by the lifestyle of the person who attempts to bear witness. Without an observable reality of lifestyle and a genuine Christlike commitment to people, the verbal witness is unconvincing.

Dr. Michael Sabo has carefully marked out the territory and has clearly set the priorities. *The Life I Want in Christ* is an unusual book that combines the best features of a spiritual treat with a delightful series of stories. Mike has chosen to share his experiences with Christ and his learning the true meaning of "abiding in Christ" through the medium of a highly personal reflection. He lets the reader into his life, his family, and his heart. In no way maudlin or cheapening, Mike's respect for the tough-minded nature of Christian spirituality shows through in every page.

Dr. Sabo has warmed a sometimes overly cold and dry topic into a delightful user-friendly reading experience. He talks about spirituality from the inside. His perspective is disarmingly subjective and real. He has been there. He has done it. Best of all, he continues faithfully to walk his spirituality as one who truly "abides in Christ."

The book sparkles with appropriate gems from the Bible. Even the Appendix is a series of well organized foundational clusters of scripture that reveal the inspired backbone of Biblical content for the entire book. Mike has been careful to let God's Word provide the compass and the flow of his story. Toward the end it becomes clear that the reader has walked painlessly along a well-marked trail toward a carefully formed theology of Christian living.

It is unlikely that any reader, no matter the level of spiritual maturity, will come away from this reading untouched.

Ted Ward
Professor Emeritus of Education and International Studies
Trinity Evangelical Divinity School
Michigan State University

Introduction

I had not seen Sue since she received her doctorate in medicine and I really looked forward to our time together. Sue and I met at a local Wendy's restaurant and we began to catch up on each other's life for the years that had passed by. She said that she was leading a Bible Study, sharing her faith with others, and was actively memorizing Scripture while being consistent in a daily quiet time. But then she mentioned a problem I understood very well: "Mike, I'm doing all the right things, but I don't sense a closeness with the Lord. What is wrong with me?"

If Sue would have told me this story five years earlier I would have said, "Sue, keep doing what you're doing and I'm sure that eventually you'll feel close to the Lord"–and I would have totally failed to understand the real point of her concern and distress. However, having experienced the same longing for intimacy with God that sometimes does not come from doing the various spiritual disciplines, I understood what she was experiencing.

I sadly smiled and said to Sue, "I know why you feel this way. You are simply doing what I taught you, but it will not necessarily produce intimacy with God. Let me tell you what I am learning about experiencing the intimacy with Christ that the Bible describes as *abiding in Christ*." As I explained about abiding in Christ and how intimacy with God can be cultivated in one's life, she began to verbally sigh and with tears in her eyes said, "I can do that. I want that."

Can you relate to Sue? I have helped many men and women to function well outwardly, but who inwardly really longed for *intimacy* with Christ. I had really missed the point of what all of the spiritual disciplines were designed to foster.

I remember being forced to think about discipleship quite differently after completing the second year on my doctoral studies. It was Christmas break and my wife, Darlene, and I decided to pack our four children into the car and head for Pennsylvania to visit our parents.

We had traveled about three hours and, after the excitement of the trip had worn off and the first fight was settled, there was peace and quiet in the Sabo station wagon. Darlene and the children had fallen asleep and I was savoring the sweet tranquility that filled the air. After enjoying about thirty minutes of the quiet, I decided to play our *Praise Album* cassette by The Bill Gaither Trio.[1] The Gaithers have ministered greatly to me and my family over the years and not much time had passed when a familiar and favorite song of mine, "It Is Finished," began to play.

There's a line that's been drawn through the ages,
On that line stands an old rugged cross;
On the cross a battle is raging,
For the gain of man's soul or his loss.

On one side march the forces of evil,
All the demons and devils of Hell;
On the other the angels of glory,
And they meet on Golgotha's hill.

The earth shakes with the force of the conflict,
And the sun refuses to shine;
For there hangs God's Son in the balance,
And then through the darkness He cries.

It is finished, the battle is over,
It is finished, there'll be no more war;
It is finished, the end of the conflict,
It is finished, and Jesus is Lord.

Still in my heart the battle was raging,
Not all pris'ners of war have come home;
There were battlefields of my own making,
I didn't know that the war had been won.

Then I heard that the King of the Ages,
Had fought all the battles for me;
And that vict'ry was mine for the claiming,
And now, Praise His Name, I am free.

It is finished, the battle is over,
It is finished, there'll be no more war;
It is finished, the end of the conflict,
It is finished, and Jesus is Lord.

While listening to the song, a question entered my mind: "What is finished?" As the song continued I received the answer. I was told that because Jesus is Lord, the war against evil and sin has been won and the war is over. The battle is finished and I can stop striving to fight the battle and live free in Christ. But the song continues and indicates that there are some who are not aware that "It is finished, the battle is over." This lack of awareness can certainly refer to the unbeliever, but I wondered, "Why are there so many Christians who do not appear to be living a life of freedom and intimacy with Christ?" Even now as I reflect on this song, many people like Sue come to mind who are doing all the 'right' activities but who do not have an intimate relationship with Christ.

These two incidents highlight at least two problems facing many Christians today. First, we tend to view particular activities – prayer, Bible study, Scripture memorization, witnessing, meditation and quiet times, Sunday worship, etc. – as more spiritual than others. Second, we tend to focus on making disciples (the Great Commission) at the expense of loving God (the Great Commandment). *What would life be like if we experienced Christ in all of what we do instead of just parts of what we do? Would ministry be different if we consciously lived in the presence of God throughout the day?*

Few Christians live in a way that indicates that "the King of the Ages" has already fought all the battles and is reigning victorious. This victory, however, must be continually affirmed. We *are* free! We are *free* to know the living God in intimate relationship through Jesus Christ. So we need not live in bondage to some kind of mechanical lifestyle articulated by many sincere believers I was one of them – which consists of maintaining certain rules, behaviors, and activities as the primary marks of maturity and ministry. The performance model of Christian living completely misses the power, the freedom of the Gospel of Jesus Christ.

§§§

This book has grown out of many mistakes I have made in my own walk with the Lord while I also was trying to minister for Him. It has a twofold thrust. The first thrust starts with where we all begin spiritually: lost and in need of salvation. I assume that every person in every part of his or her being – mind, spirit, soul, body, emotions, motives, etc. – is corrupted by sin. Theologians call this corruption by sin "total depravity." It means that through all of time every person in every aspect of his or her being is born marred by and under the control of sin. Thus, I assume that everyone through all of time in every aspect of his or her humanity is in need of healing from the effects of sin and freedom from its control: salvation in Jesus Christ. The second thrust examines why many Christians do not enjoy and experience their freedom in Christ or their relationship with God. It is here where Christ's teaching on *abiding* (John 15) is examined and shown to be the foundation for maturity and the ministry to others rather than the keeping of particular activities or disciplines.

My prayer is that you understand what it means to be free in Christ in your whole being as you discover and begin to experience the *life* you want in Christ.

Notes

[1] William J. Gaither, Praise Album (Impact Records, 1965)

SECTION ONE

The Problem — Darkness

CHAPTER 1

A Bright New House

My children enjoy making cookies, particularly at Christmas time, and I enjoy a good cookie with a hot cup of herbal tea as I sit and look up at the sparkles and colors of our Christmas tree, even though it's artificial. This led to an interesting discovery one Christmas. When my two oldest daughters make cookies, the ginger bread men look identical, the stars are virtual blueprints of each other, and the cross-shaped cookies have all the same markings. How can this be? I uncovered the truth that my children's artistic abilities are not quite as great as I thought. I came into the kitchen one evening and there before my eyes, right out in the open where everyone could see, was a cookie cutter! This simple little utensil made it very easy to produce identical cookies quickly.

The cookie cutter is a great idea for making cookies, but not for making disciples. For unlike cookie dough, people possess individual characteristics and traits that must be studied, considered, and appreciated if we hope to make disciples who follow Christ. If our desire is to focus on a preconceived program or manual that tells us how we should make disciples, then we may become one of the greatest hindrances to a young Christian's maturity. Sincere people who simply do all the right activities yet lack a deep abiding walk with Christ are not mature disciples, nor will they grow as they could.

Recently I was listening to a Christian radio program with two prominent Christian leaders being interviewed. The interviewer was asking one of the individuals to articulate the differences between mentoring and discipleship. When the respondent described discipleship, he said that "discipleship is the passing on of spiritual disciplines" (e.g., prayer, Bible study, etc.). I wondered where he got that definition! When I study Scripture, I do not see Jesus rallying people to do activities, even those activities society views as spiritual or holy. As a matter of fact, Jesus strongly rebuked the Pharisees for embracing empty behavior. He said to them, "Woe to you, scribes and Pharisees, hypocrites! For you are like whitewashed tombs which on the outside appear beautiful, but inside they are full of dead men's bones and all uncleanness. Even so you too outwardly appear righteous to men, but inwardly you are full of hypocrisy and lawlessness" (Matthew 23:27-28). It seems Jesus was not content with uniting people around outward activities, disciplines, and behavior; rather He revealed that real, authentic Christianity and discipleship revolves around an inner relationship with the Father.

Often I speak with pastors and other Christian leaders who, although aware of the problems in getting people to do activities in and of themselves, are frustrated when it comes to helping people obey the word of God. In frustration, they often resort to breaking a person up into parts thereby losing sight of the whole-person. The most common part focused upon is the mind. As a result, the myth that "to know is sufficient" gets promoted from the pulpit and accepted in the pew. In other words, if we know something intellectually, then our lifestyle will change. This myth must be rejected. We can't grow apart from God's Word, but God's Word is to be applied to all of our being if growth is to occur. When we disciple people by helping them to grow and to contribute within God's kingdom, they must be trained with more than just their minds in view. This myth is often encouraged by discipleship training and programs. But discipleship that breaks a person up into parts and then focuses upon one part as more important falls far short of the Great Commission:

> And Jesus came up and spoke to them, saying, "All authority has been given to Me in heaven and on earth. Go therefore and make disciples of all the nations, baptizing them in the name of the Father and the Son and the Holy Spirit, *teaching them to observe* all that I commanded you; and lo, I am with you always, even to the end of the age." (Matthew 28:18-20)

Here we see that Jesus' commission entails teaching people to live the truth, not just place it in their minds. Teaching people to obey cannot be accomplished if all we have to work with is their minds. We are more than just a brain on a stick! A *whole-person perspective* is needed which includes not only our minds but our whole being.

Working part-time in a health club I am often amused to observe body builders who possess massive upper torsos supported by legs that look like tooth picks. Too often these athletes do not understand the need to develop their entire bodies. The danger of this type of training is that due to an imbalance in their training, injury can occur very easily. A holistic approach focusing on each area of the body gives balance, strength, and soundness to the whole-body. This same principle of whole-body training should be applied to the Great Commission if we are to keep in step with Christ's whole-person redemption through *whole-person discipleship.*

To further explain what I mean by whole-person discipleship, the rest of this chapter is spent presenting a framework for better understanding ourselves and for ministering to the whole-person.

The Whole Person

I grew up in a small town in eastern Pennsylvania called Slabtown. It is forty-five minutes south of Williamsport, Pa., where the Little League World Series is held. Slabtown at that time had a population of only two hundred people. Many of the homes there were two story in design. The house I grew up in was very much like the one pictured below. The front door was centrally located on the first floor with a win-

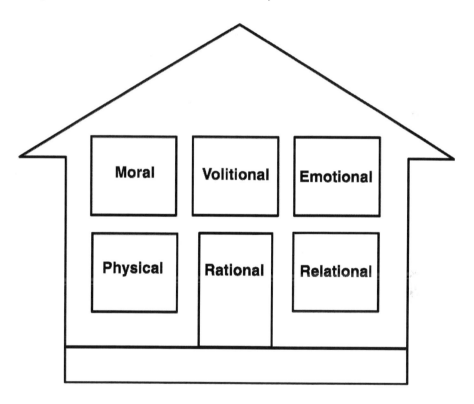

dow on each side, while the second floor had three windows straight across.

This "house illustration" can help us understand the primary dimensions of what it is to be human. So imagine that this house represents my life in its fullest sense. The door represents the entrance to the rational domain of my humanity where the beliefs, attitudes, and values by which I function are held. The windows represent the physical, moral, volitional, emotional, and relational dimensions of my life and they serve as the means by which others can practically observe what I truly believe. Put another way, you really do not come to know what the interior is like through the door because the real beliefs, attitudes, and values are revealed inside the house. But even if I do not permit you to come through the door and into my home, you can still attempt to gain a better understanding of the interior of my life by looking through the windows of my life.

Please keep in mind that this entire book is written to practically assist you in sensing the presence of God in all of your being and to help others do the same. Therefore, chapters one and two tend to be a little technical and theoretical. These two chapters provide the basis for the practical experience of intimacy with Christ, which is explained in the remaining eight chapters.

Let's examine in some detail first the function of the door, our rational dimension, and then the various windows which reveal the other aspects of our being.

The Door: Entrance to Our Rational Dimension

If you were to visit my home to take a poll on various social, religious, or political issues, you could simply knock on my door, I would answer, and you could begin to ask me questions. Your intent is to determine what I, the owner of this home, think and believe. However, since I do not know you or anything about you, I may not trust you or I may be afraid of how you might respond to me if I really told you what goes on inside of my house. And I may even get defensive.

Once when I was speaking to a group of church elders and pastors, one elder said that he was an architect. He mentioned that a phrase often used in architecture is 'defensible space.' He explained that defensible space refers to the area surrounding a residence within which only a few select people are welcome without being viewed as intruders. This space varies from residence to residence, but it is usually considered to be the front yard or front porch of the house.

If a mail carrier enters this space, the owner of the home would not take offense. However, if a stranger entered the front yard or appeared on the porch uninvited, the home owner might take offense and embrace a defensive attitude. The concept of defensible space is like the defensive posture we take with many people, particularly when we are identifying our beliefs, attitudes, and values. These are things we consider to be private and not generally available for public knowledge uninvited. Let's turn this around and look at it for disciplemaking. If we think that we can directly address another's personal issues (their beliefs, attitudes, or values) without developing a relationship with him or her and being invited to do so, we will most likely find resistance and defensiveness. The person is just defending private space. This would probably not be the best approach in ministering to people.

I teach two martial arts, Jujutsu and Tae Kwon Do, as a means of income and ministry contacts. Tae Kwon Do emphasizes kicks and punches while Jujutsu uses pressure points, arm bars, and wrist locks to subdue an attacker. Suppose I came up to you and placed your wrist in such a position that you experienced great pain. While showing you my latest technique I ask, "Do you think I'm better than Chuck Norris (a well-known martial artist and movie actor)?" As you contemplate the question you sense increasing pain shooting up your arm as I apply pressure to your wrist. You reply, "Yes! Oh, Chuck would not stand a chance against you!" However, you are saying to yourself, "Ha, better than Chuck Norris? You would stand a better chance of running across Lake Michigan than beating Norris!"

This imaginary scenario reveals that beliefs like our motives frequently cannot be directly observed but must be implied through what we say and do and, therefore, can be easily misinterpreted and misunderstood. *Beliefs* are inferences, not, necessarily things we affirm with our lips.[1] Just because I say things with my mouth ("I believe this" or "I believe that") does not mean that such statements are my true beliefs. As you watch my life, you can (and do!) infer from my actions what my true beliefs are. We must realize that there are many reasons, such as fear, pride, and deception, which keep us from stating our true beliefs.[2]

An *attitude* is the organization of several beliefs focused onto a specific person, circumstance, or object which predisposes a person to respond in a particular manner.[3] For example, you may have a particular bias about martial artists. You may believe that they all train in the Orient for years, break ice, wood, and steel with their bare hands, have their hands and feet registered with the FBI, and had to kill ten people to get their black belt. Your attitude could be summed up in the phrase "Don't mess with them!"

A *value* is a single belief that serves as a standard for other beliefs and attitudes. Values guide our beliefs and attitudes while helping us to evaluate and justify ourselves and others. Values are necessary to actions. For example, suppose someone said, "I believe that avoiding physical pain is personally and socially preferable in all situations."[4] Remembering our earlier martial arts scenario, in that situation the respondent ("you") chose to lie to avoid further physical pain rather than express his ("your") true belief.

To summarize, if I do not let you come through the door and into my house, all you can do is attempt to understand my beliefs, attitudes, and values by what you see through the windows of my house. In addition, depending on how close I let you come to my house, you may or may not be able to see clearly or accurately through the windows of my house.

Windows: Looking into Our Physical Dimension

Usually when we encounter someone for the first time (apart from a letter or phone conversation), we see them physically. I recently met a new member of our athletic club who is a very good racquetball player. He is tall, quick, with good hand/eye coordination, and shoots the ball like a cannon. I have become his student not only to play against him on the racquetball court but more importantly to learn how God designed him in order to move closer to him as a friend. We should be a student not only of the mind but also of the physical qualities and abilities of the people we want to know.

Below is a list of some elements of our bodies which can be helpful in learning about the physical qualities of others: hygiene, diet, sleep, exercise, clothing, flexibility, height, weight, muscle mass, density and tone, hand/eye coordination, balance, strength, body proportion, skin color, eye and hair color. These are only a few of the physical characteristics that God has given to mankind. Being aware of these qualities in others can help us build bridges and develop relationships.

Windows: Looking into Our Moral Dimension

The moral dimension of our humanity is the standard by which we live. Anytime we say something is good or bad, right or wrong, better or best, we are revealing a portion of our standards. When we evaluate a given task or job and give our opinion on the quality of the work, we are revealing or at least referring to our standards for workmanship or craftsmanship. As students submit assignments required to pass the courses I teach, I place a grade on their papers along with comments on their insights and depth of thought. The assigned grade and comments are a reflection of my standards.

As I write this chapter I am drinking a mug of basic herbal tea. This is a good cup of tea when I compare it to a general black tea. But when I compare it to peach herbal tea, this cup of tea is not very good. The cup of tea I am drinking has not changed, but the standard by which it is compared has changed and the evaluation is different. We are beings who regularly interact and evaluate people and the circumstances of life, and are thereby revealing our standards.

As we spend time with individuals we need to observe their standards of life. What do they consider to be good or bad? What do they qualify as beautiful or ugly? Are their standards of right and wrong unbending, sometimes flexible, or always changing direction like the wind? Our moral dimension reveals our beliefs, attitudes, and values.

Windows: Looking into Our Volitional Dimension

Our volitional dimension, is expressed in our ability to make choices. These choices are based on our beliefs, attitudes, and values; but the ability to choose is different from mere instinct. Theologians and philosophers refer to our volitional dimension as "the will."

I find it particularly fascinating to watch my son Ben play basketball. Ben and I have regular interaction in his bedroom over basketball games and dart throwing. We have selected two trophies that are designated "basketball" and "darts." We routinely play a basketball game called "horse." Each of us is required to make the same shot as our opponent makes. If, however, my son makes a shot and I miss it, then I receive one letter in the word "horse." The loser is the first one to receive all the letters of the word "horse."

Ben's hero is Chicago Bulls basketball player, Michael Jordan. If you have ever watched Jordan play basketball, you have seen some phenomenal shooting. My son studies Jordan's shots and those of other pro basketball players, and writes them down for reference. He then brings them to our "horse" playoffs! There is a lot of joking around as Ben and I attempt to make various shots. I'll ask Ben, "Why did you make that shot?" He'll respond, "Jordan likes that shot" or "Because you can't make that shot, Dad!" Needless to say, I have only won the basketball trophy one time.

My son is a volitional being. He is a young man who is actively choosing to make decisions that move him in directions to achieve particular goals, desires, and accomplishments. *The choices people make are of tremendous value in learning what is important to them.* Study the people God has placed around you in order to effectively influence them for Christ.

Windows: Looking into Our Emotional Dimension

Webster defines emotion as, "the physical reactions to subjective experiences that involve strong feelings and physiological reactions that prepare the body for a type of action."[5] Most of us can easily identify the times we expressed emotions we are fond of and those times we wish an emotion would never have been expressed.

My wife, Darlene, and I enjoy going to the movies or watching a home video. We have identified two elements that we look for in a movie: Darlene looks for romance and I look for action. We will often describe a movie as 60% romance and 40% action. I never cease to be amazed that I get excited when I see action on the screen and Darlene turns in the other direction. But when the romantic stuff comes on I feel unmoved and disinterested and I start looking for the popcorn. Why Darlene sheds tears over some of the things that come on the screen is still a mystery to me; however, I'm learning quickly.

Darlene is really different from me, and if I am to develop a meaningful relationship with her, I must be aware of her emotional states and realize that her emotional makeup is legitimate and simply different from mine. I have learned that different doesn't necessarily mean wrong.

Windows: Looking into Our Relational Dimension

1	2
3	4

As a child lying in bed, I often looked out of the window in my bedroom. It was made of four separate glass panes. Our relational dimension has four components that make up the whole.

One pane represents *how we relate to ourselves.* In other words, how do we really view ourselves? What do we think and say about ourselves?

I have really come to enjoy teaching Tae Kwon Do to children four years of age and older. In the 12-17 year old group I have a wide variety of personalities and abilities. Recently, a young student approached me and announced that he was now ready to spar with me, his instructor. He was not coming as a learner to be taught and refine techniques, but was arrogantly announcing that he was now ready for tournament fighting with his instructor. In the same class I have a student who is very quiet and shy and who tends to question his ability and proficiency quite often. He becomes fearful of new situations and often wants to excuse himself from participation because of a sore finger or an upset stomach. Each of these individuals view themselves, at least in my Tae Kwon Do class, in very different ways. One may be over confident thinking that, "Once I get past my instructor, Chuck Norris is next." By contrast, the more timid student would question his ability to break Jell-O and, therefore, become suddenly ill when it's time to break a one-inch board.

Another perspective with regard to the way we view ourselves relates to how we view human nature. Do we see human nature as good that can or cannot change? Or do we view human nature as evil that can or cannot be altered? Or do we view human nature as neutral, being able to choose good or evil?

If you want to minister to others, we must do it in light of their individual tendencies. If we do not see the value in observing others' view of themselves, we will probably miss many opportunities to draw others closer to the Lord. We need to learn through observation and to clarify through questions. We must pray that the Spirit of God will give us unique insights into how we can minister effectively.

The second pane of the relational window is *how we relate to others.* There are a number of questions that will aid in understanding this dimension. Does this individual tend to be individualistic and a lone wolf? Does he view relationships more in a linear manner by only using individuals to benefit himself? Or does he take more of a team approach and see relationships as opportunities to give and receive? More specifically, how does he treat his mate and children? How does the senior pastor treat the church staff? How does the seminary professor treat students in class? The answers to these questions and many more like them are a reflection of the relational window of how we and others relate to our fellow human beings.

Do we really treat others as more important than ourselves? While working at an athletic facility, I was approached by a member who became angry that a group had reserved part of the gym floor for badminton. He was unwilling to see that they were paying members just as he was and that they had followed club procedures in reserving the floor and therefore had a right to use that floor, too. He attempted to make fun of them because he did not get what he wanted. It was obvious that the way this individual responded to me revealed how he relates to others and how he views himself.

The third pane of the relational window pertains to *how we relate to creation.* Let me illustrate this dimension by a hypothetical situation. One year ago we purchased a used VW Jetta. It was a nice car even though it was used. If I asked, "what do you think about my car?" and you responded by scratching the hood with a nail, your action would communicate not only what you think about my car but, more importantly, what you think about me.

While walking across the campus of Trinity Evangelical Divinity School, I have often seen candy wrappers on the ground. Assuming that they did not blow out of the trash barrel, I wondered what the individuals were thinking when they littered. Were they thinking that the maintenance department would pick up the wrappers? Did they think about how this action reflects upon their view of the seminary staff, administration, and the student body? More importantly, did they contemplate that their activity was an expression of how they view the Creator and owner of planet earth? Thinking about this in a broader sense, how do these students view nature?

This window-pane also includes an understanding of their responsibility toward creation. Do they see human beings as *masters* over the universe studying and analyzing it with conquering it as their goal? Do they see themselves as *stewards* having the authority to control and have dominion over the environment? Perhaps they are more comfortable with viewing themselves as *subjects* to nature and that whatever happens happens, and therefore they cannot and should not do anything to stop or interfere with the forces of nature. They see themselves as having no control over or any responsibility toward their environment, but are simply respondents to their surroundings. Or do they describe themselves as *harmonizers* with nature attempting to work with creation. If so, their intent is not to control nature or to act as a non-interfering agent, but rather to see humanity's responsibility as working alongside the forces of the universe.

An individual's perspective on the use of time can also reveal how he views creation. Time is indeed a part of God's creation, but it will not exist in heaven as we understand and experience time on earth. With regard to our earthly residence, however, how do the individuals we are attempting to learn about view time? Does he or she see time as a resource to be appreciated and not abused? Or does he or she tend to live life without any apparent awareness of the passage of time?

We need to observe how people treat the creation of God. These observations can be a practical and helpful means of entering more deeply into the lives of others.

The final pane in the relational window highlights *how we relate to God.* Humans, unlike all other created beings, have the privileged opportunity to relate to the Creator of the universe as Father. Examine how others talk and think about God. Do they view themselves as agnostics believing that they lack sufficient information to make a decision about the existence of God? Do they describe themselves as atheistic believing that they have enough information and sufficient evidence that God does not exist? Or do they view God in some pantheistic manner believing that "god" is everything? Are they more comfortable with polytheism, the belief that there are many distinct deities? Or is monotheism their choice and they believe in the existence of only one God.

Regardless of their perspective, ask questions to learn about them (not questions that indict) and remember what they say. God will take the everyday experiences you and others share to deepen your friendships while giving you many opportunities to sow and water (more on these two terms later) effectively.

What? No Spiritual Window?

Some of you might be saying that you were aware of these dimensions through your studies of the social sciences and, therefore, you are asking, "So, what's new?" Being a Christian, you have come to learn that there is a dimension that is spiritual that the secular humanist omits and often denies.

I do not believe that we possess a spiritual dimension. Instead I believe that we are by God's design spiritual beings and that our spirituality is manifested through all of life. To relate my point to the house illustration, spirituality is not a part of being a human. We are by nature spiritual beings. Scripture indicates it this way: we are either spiritually alive or spiritually dead (Romans 3). The important point to remember is that our true spirituality or lack of it will be seen through these windows. So whether we teach martial arts, go to a movie, lead a Bible study, or change a dirty diaper, we are to do all these things to the glory of God (1 Corinthians 10:31).

There is a tendency for us to focus upon just one of the windows and to make that an idol or the primary manifestation of our spirituality. In seminary the primary focus is the rational dimension. Lip service is given to some of the other dimensions, but very little is done to develop the whole-person. The myth promoted in many seminaries and churches throughout the United States is that *to know is sufficient,* knowing in the sense of accumulating facts. But it appears that what God is calling us to is not knowing about Him, but rather to knowing Him intimately. The danger is that we emphasize one part of our humanity as being more important than another. When we take this approach to discipleship, we are compartmentalizing our human nature and are preparing people to experience a weak and shallow Christianity. Throughout this book I will be advocating that discipleship must be focused on *whole-person development,* not only as important but as necessary if we are to be faithful to our Lord's teaching. We must *observe all that he has commanded,* as stated in the Great Commission (Matthew 28:18-20), and pay heed to the Lord's Great Commandment: "'You shall love the LORD your God with all your heart, and with all your soul, and with all your mind.' This is the great and foremost commandment" (Matthew 22:37-38).

Summary

I have shown that there is more to people than their mental capacities. If we are to be students of others, we must learn to study the windows of people's lives. By being meticulous students of the dimensions of human beings – the physical, moral, volitional, emotional, and relational – we can learn the true beliefs, attitudes, and values of others and will be far better equipped to let the word of God shine through in *relevant* ways into each person's life. We need to remember that the purpose of looking in through the windows of a person's life is to learn who the person is, not to judge him or her. We should attempt to identify those qualities in each person, which are desirable and seek ministry opportunities to build upon these qualities. As Proverbs 24:3-4 records, "By wisdom a house is built, and by understanding it is established; and by knowledge the rooms are filled with all precious and pleasant riches."

In my teenage years I spent quite a bit of time at my father's service station. Many times I wanted to be out playing ball, but through the years I have grown to be thankful for all that I have learned about working on cars. My father's instruction and training have proven to be very valuable. Automobile maintenance can be challenging. These days, however, with the on-board multiple computer systems of the newer model cars, car repair has become a science. If, for example, you are working on the fuel system of a car but you possess no understanding of the automobile's ignition system, this ignorance could turn out to be expensive and frustrating, particularly if you believe that in order to get the car to run all you have to do is simply get fuel to the carburetor. Without proper spark, there is no way for the fuel to be ignited and the automobile will not run. Similarly, since people consist of more than just a body and a mind, we must remember their *whole-person* as we teach them to obey our heavenly Father.

Notes

[1] Milton Rokeach, *Belief, Attitudes, and Values* (San Francisco, Ca.: Jossey-Bass, 1986), p. 2.

[2] Ibid.

[3] Ibid., p. 159.

[4] Ibid., p. 160.

[5] *Webster's Seventh New Collegiate Dictionary* (Springfield: G. & C. Merriam Company, 1969), p. 271.

CHAPTER 2

A Darkened, Unstable House

"There is none righteous, not even one;
there is none who understands,
there is none who seeks for God;
all have turned aside, together they have become
useless; there is none who does good, there is not even one.
Their throat is an open grave,
with their tongues they keep deceiving,
The poison of asps is under their lips";
Whose mouth is full of cursing and bitterness;
Their feet are swift to shed blood,
destruction and misery are in their paths,
and the path of peace have they not known.
There is no fear of God before their eyes."

— Romans 3:10-18 —

Humanity's Miserable State

The book of Genesis describes mankind as the supreme creation of God's creative activity. Yet, as we watch the nightly news and read the daily newspapers it appears that humanity is also the object of supreme misery and failure.

Adam's first sin planted the seed of depravity in the human race touching every part of every person. Every dimension and faculty of our existence has been marred by sin. Such total depravity, however, does not mean that we are in our worst possible state, but that all of what and who we are has been tainted by sin. Our condition can be compared to an individual who has been dipped into hot tar. The individual still has functioning arms and legs, yet the movement and use of his entire body is directly affected by the scalding affects of the tar. To get a closer look at how Scripture describes mankind's corruption, take a look at Genesis 6:5; Psalm 14:3; and Romans 7:18.

One devastating effect of sin is its enslaving power. This is seen by the multiplying effects of sin. Consider Cain and Abel and how uncontrolled anger leads to murder which leads to lying (Genesis 4:1-15). Consider Abraham's continual lies about Sarah as he attempts to pass her off as his sister not his wife (Genesis 12:10-20). Consider David's tragic road of sin with Bathsheba and Uriah and how lust becomes rape, cover-ups beget lies, and deception develops into murder (2 Samuel 11-12). Enslaving can be compared to addiction. Even though the addict realizes that his habit is tearing his marriage and family to pieces, there seems to be something mysteriously drawing him to indulge his habit just one more time. There is a strange element to sin that is difficult to understand, but nonetheless is real and able to be overcome.

As shown in Chapter 1, the house illustration portrays a whole-person perspective of an individual. Before we begin to take a closer look at how whole-person discipleship can occur, we must first understand how Adam's fall from God's grace has stamped mankind totally, keeping in mind that we must have a proper understanding of sin in order to be effective in the whole-person discipling process to which the Lord has called us.

Upon examination, we see that there are at least six different but interwoven dimensions of an individual's humanity. Even though I talk about these as separate aspects, the individual is a combination of them all. Man's dimensions consist of the rational, physical, moral, volitional, emotional, and relational which, have all been influenced by the Fall. This total person marring of man is implicit in Scripture but not thoroughly explicit. Whole-person depravity will be further explained as we review a few relevant passages of Scripture which reveal how each dimension is flawed and needs restoration.

The Door: Our Rational Depravity

We must understand that our thinking capacity still functions since the Fall but it is the accuracy that is marred and distorted. If we inaccurately evaluate ourselves, our actions will most likely follow how we think about ourselves. If for example, I think I can fly my thinking abilities are functioning however my conclusion is inaccurate. This will become evident if I jump from an airplane without a parachute. Therefore, an accurate view of our thoughts is critical to understanding why we behave and feel as we do. Consider the following six biblical examples of depravity at the rational level.

Tower of Babel (Genesis 11) – In this narrative there appears to be faulty thinking in regard to who they are and who the Lord is.

Mind Is Blinded (2 Corinthians 4:4) – Here we see that the mind has been blinded by the enemy so that people may not see the light of the gospel.

Learning and Truth Are Not The Same (2 Timothy 3:7) – The apostle Paul further identifies mankind's problem in which he says, "always learning and never able to come to the knowledge of the truth."

Renewed Mind Needed (Romans 12:2) – Paul understood that the mind needs to be liberated from the bonds of sin. He indicates that every Christian must have a "renewed mind."

Man's Wisdom Is Foolishness to God (Romans 1:21-22) – This passage is further evidence that we are living in darkness and futility, for our very wisdom is the epitome of foolishness.

Worship Things Rather Than God (Romans 1:25) – Here Paul reveals that we have traded the truth for a lie and have chosen to worship the created rather than the Creator. This is evidence of a twisted and distorted dimension of mankind which needs liberation. In order to honor God for who He is, our rational dimension must be freed from the captivating grip of sin.

Our rational dimension (beliefs, attitudes, and values) is manifested in the way we live. Our living can be understood as we reflect upon the way we take care of our body (physical), the standards we live by (moral), the choices we make (volitional), the emotions we experience (emotional), and the relationships we have with ourselves, others, creation, and God (relational). All of these dimensions are networked to the rational dimension. Our attitudes, values, and beliefs (rational) are expressed throughout our entire lives. We can quickly see that the state of our minds will have direct influence upon our entire being. In other words, what we truly believe (not just verbalize) will be lived and seen in the windows of our lives (house illustration).

Romans 1 reveals not only a whole-person view of mankind but also a frightening picture of our total depravity. Verse 21 particularly describes the darkened state of man's mind. Verse 28 informs us that when an individual chooses to deny God and ignore His Lordship (just as Adam in the garden), God chooses to give the person a depraved mind. We live in a world which not only denies God's lordship and sovereign rule but even His existence! This observation is another sign of the impairment of our mental capacities.

For those interested in further study of man's mental marring please refer to Appendix A.

Windows: Our Physical Depravity

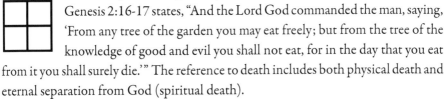 Genesis 2:16-17 states, "And the Lord God commanded the man, saying, 'From any tree of the garden you may eat freely; but from the tree of the knowledge of good and evil you shall not eat, for in the day that you eat from it you shall surely die.'" The reference to death includes both physical death and eternal separation from God (spiritual death).

Genesis 18 (the birth of Isaac as promised to Abraham and Sarah) describes this couple as old and Sarah having passed the age of childbearing. Here we see an example that the body ages and becomes incapable of particular functions that men and women were originally blessed with by God. We see throughout the pages of Scripture men and women suffering from physical infirmities and dying of disease and old age. It is a sad picture when contrasted to the original state of Adam and Eve prior to their choice to rebel against God.

Recently I watched the movie *Awakenings* with Robert De Niro and Robin Williams. This beautiful movie, based on a true story, portrayed Robin Williams in the role of Dr. Malcolm Sayer, a shy research physician who treated catatonic victims with an experimental drug. As the patients awoke from their catatonic state, Dr. Sayer began to develop friendships with each. But a special friendship developed between him and Leonard (Robert De Niro). As Leonard later began to regress, expressed by severe bodily jerking and difficult speech, I became overwhelmed and wept. I was reminded that what I was observing was due to sin. We are sick and in need of healing.

So infectious is our individual sin that it can be found in all strata of life, from the ghettos of any of our major cities to the White House. Not long ago I saw the movie *JFK*. I do not claim that what I viewed was a true representation of the facts; however, the film portrayed graphic physical expressions of sin initiated at a corporate level. According to the plot, major governmental agencies conspired together to bring about the assassination of John F. Kennedy.

We are not only in need of deliverance of our individual sin, but we also need a King to deliver us from all types of sin!

If you are interested in further study in regard to the physical dimension refer to Appendix B.

Windows: Our Moral Depravity

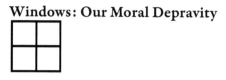

Morality springs from principles that enable us to distinguish right from wrong. Anytime we evaluate something as good or bad, right or wrong, better or best we are expressing our standards. We live in a society with standards that are constantly changing because people have embraced self-serving morals rather than the uncompromising standards of God (found in Scripture) which are for His glory and our best.

A Biblical example of moral depravity very familiar to many people is the story of Sodom and Gomorrah (Genesis 18:16-19:29). The Lord tells Abraham that he is going to destroy the cities due to their sin. Abraham's nephew Lot (and his family) lives in the city, so Abraham strikes a bargain with the Lord:

> Wilt Thou indeed sweep away the righteous with the wicked? Suppose there are fifty righteous within the city, wilt Thou indeed sweep it away and not spare the place for the sake of the fifty righteous who are in it? Far be it from Thee to do such a thing, to slay the righteous with the wicked, so that the righteous and the wicked are treated alike. Far be it from Thee! Shall not the Judge of the whole earth deal justly? So the Lord said, "If I find in Sodom fifty righteous within the city, then I will spare the whole place on their account." (Genesis 18:23-26)

Having gained this much, Abraham bargains for forty-five, then thirty, and then twenty. Each time, the Lord agrees not to destroy the cities for the sake of the righteous. Abraham then bargains for ten, the Lord agrees and then departs from Abraham's presence – end of discussion.

Meanwhile at the entrance gate to Sodom, Lot intercepts two angels coming into the city who planned on sleeping in the town square, and urged them to stay in his home so strongly that they finally agreed. The men of Sodom want Lot to turn over his guests to them so that they could "have [sexual] relations with them" (Genesis 19:5). Lot pleads with them:

Please, my brothers, do not act wickedly. Now behold, I have two daughters who have not had relations with man; please let me bring them out to you, and do with them whatever you like, only do nothing to these men, inasmuch as they have come under the shelter of my roof. (Genesis 19:7-8) The men of Sodom refused Lot's virginal daughters, commanded him to stand aside and let them enter his home to seize the "men" angels for sex, and they began to abuse Lot for protecting his guests and for "acting like a judge" toward them, the Sodomites. The angels saved Lot by blinding the men of Sodom who eventually "wearied themselves trying to find the door." (Genesis 19:9-10)

What is amazing about this whole story is that even though the wickedness of Sodom and Gomorrah is obvious to both Abraham and Lot, they are reluctant to see them destroyed. Lot is so ambivalent; first he offers his daughters to be sexually abused and then hesitates to leave the next day. He is so ambivalent that the angels literally seize and drag him out of the city, for not even ten righteous could be found and the Lord was ready to destroy not only the cities but the entire valley.

It seems that when principles for living are not drawn from the pages of Scripture, mankind's justification for behavior shifts as quickly as the flight path of a humming bird, which quickly darts north, south, east, and west serving the desires of the creature. This example reminds me of Judges 17:6: "In those days there was no king in Israel; every man did what was right in his own eyes." Here we find people who had no ruler to give them direction so they decided to do what they deemed right. The context of Judges 17 depicts people who lived with no absolute standards; some even made and worshipped idols. This story could easily be contextualized today with replacing the idol made out of silver with cars, houses, clothing, etc. The list is virtually endless. When we must make decisions we all need standards to turn to in order to determine our actions. People of today are no different from those of Judges 17; their morals have been sabotaged by the Fall and in need of desperate repair.

Further study in this dimension can be found in Appendix C.

Windows: Our Volitional Depravity

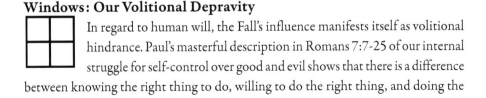 In regard to human will, the Fall's influence manifests itself as volitional hindrance. Paul's masterful description in Romans 7:7-25 of our internal struggle for self-control over good and evil shows that there is a difference between knowing the right thing to do, willing to do the right thing, and doing the

right thing. *Knowing has to do with content; willing with will (the volitional); and doing with the power needed to obey.*[1]

Paul indicates that he takes responsibility for the sinful activity he performs even though the sinful act is against his will. One might be led to believe that Paul is saying that since the sinful activity is against his will ("if I do what I do not want to do") he is not responsible. This conclusion is not true. Paul announced that even though he ended up doing what he did not want to do he was still the acting agent doing the sinful activity and was therefore accountable. Romans 7:25 indicates that Paul was taking responsibility for his sinful act even though the act was against his will.

The primary point is not to determine if Paul was guilty of an act that he did not will to do, but rather that there is something strangely wrong with our volition; that is, our capacity to choose. Verse 22 shows that Paul's will was frustrated by the indwelling sin that we all possess. He ended up doing what he did not want to do. Yet he says he had the desire to do what was right but he was unable to carry it out (verse 18).

Paul describes himself as a typical slave who performed the will of his master not willingly but in a more mechanical sense. He ended up carrying out the very activity he hated and what he wanted in his life never materialized.[2] However, Paul gives the solution for the Christian in Romans 7:25-8:1.

The Christian must be willing to do what is right before the power comes to do it. But according to Paul even the capacity of choice has in a mysterious way been blemished by sin. Scripture teaches that humanity possess a free will, but the marring of our capacity to choose can be seen in our bondage to our sinful predisposition. Mankind's free will has been deeply scarred by the fall of Adam. Therefore, our free wills are in bondage to serve our sinful selves and desires. In other words, humanity is addicted to sin. Our hearts are wicked continually; therefore, our volition will freely choose in light of our hearts.

Due to Adam's sin, since our conception, mankind has a predisposition to sin. Sin is at the very core of our being. Although we have the ability to choose we can only choose from what we are – sinful. Therefore, our wills are limited to choose only that which is self serving and therefore contrary to the will of God. The nonbelievers are still free in the sense of their choices. In this sense, freedom is making a choice(s) without being coerced or manipulated by something or someone else. While determinism can be understood as all my choices have been predetermined without my consent; hence I have no real choosing. We must remember that all of our choices stem from something. No choice just happens! Each choice has its roots in something within us even though we may not be conscious of what that source may be. Every choice has been influenced or caused by something. The type of freedom a nonbeliever possesses is the ability to do what they want to do. What I want to do comes from inside of me. We, therefore, can't choose against our inner most being. Our dilemma occurs when our innermost predisposition is at odds with God's will. If our innermost predisposition is sinful then all of our free choices will be sinful and thereby oppose God. The curse of Adam which we inherited has deadened our choices to do what is pleasing to God.

Our lives are full of sinfulness. Even though our wills still function, they can only choose from what is within our lives. Since our lives are full of sinfulness, our choices can only be sinful.

The very wills of mankind, our volitional capacities, have been sabotaged by the presence of sin. Our faculty of choice has been checkmated. Our ability to choose is sick; rehabilitation is necessary, and a surgeon is required.

Further study references can be found in Appendix D.

Windows: Our Emotional Depravity

The Fall's influence on our emotions may be seen in Genesis 4 in the account of Cain and Abel. Here hatred and jealousy are expressed by Cain toward Abel. While the type of anger depicted in Matthew 5:22 is really the root of murder, Ephesians 4:26 indicates that anger does not have to be sinful while warning that when we are angry we should not let it turn into sin.[3]

The decision of Adam to eat the forbidden fruit has scarred the emotional dimension of mankind. Our capacity to have and express emotion has not been eliminated but rather perverted by the presence of sin. In 1 Samuel 18 we find Saul's people dancing and singing in the street because of the victory won over the Philistines. But in verse 18, Saul became very angry when he heard the refrain of a song that indicated a greater praise for David than for himself. Saul's anger grew into jealousy and eventually resulted in attempted murder. His emotional state continued to deteriorate because he was in constant fear of David because the Lord was with David. It's important to note that many perversions of the dimensions of humanity occur when one acts as though he is independent of God and approaches life by himself.

Saul is not alone in struggling with an emotional state infected by sin. Our prisons and penitentiaries are full of those who were influenced by perverted emotional states and who have broken the law. But even more importantly, every person regardless of his or her relationship with the laws of the land has and will continue to do battle with their emotions unless there is intervention. We are totally depraved, and our emotional state has certainly not escaped the infection. Our emotional state is in need of redemption.

Additional references regarding the emotional dimension are located in Appendix E.

Windows: Our Relational Depravity

Sin's effects are also revealed in our distorted relationships. We have the capacity to have at least four types of relationships. First, we have the capacity to relate to ourselves. We all love ourselves. We care for and nurture ourselves, as best we know how. The problem with self love is that we are selfish and we care for ourselves at the expense of others. Some of us are very proud while others have very low views of themselves. Both views are wrong and both are sinful. Examples of the influence of sin on the way we view ourselves are particular types of depression, internal struggles, despair, shame, feelings of guilt, pride, lack of self worth, independence from God, perverted self love, and denial of death.

Second, we have the capacity to relate to other human beings. Our depravity is manifested in the inability to love (agape) unconditionally. The Scriptures and the morning newspapers are full of examples of men and women individually, and as a nation, not relating to each other in ways that please God. Additional examples of man at odds with his fellowman are blaming others, indifference toward others (Genesis 4:9: "Am I my brother's keeper?"), rivalry, perverted sexual relationships, hatred, unrighteous anger, bitterness, coveting, prejudice, racism, the need of police to protect us from one another, confused communication, distorted roles of men and women, and unwillingness to help the poor and needy (Galatians 5:19-21).

Third, we have the capacity to relate to creation. The way we view and respond to our surroundings is an example of this ability. The ecological problems we presently face are yet another example of the poor job we are doing in this relational calling. Further examples are a perverted view of aesthetics which inhibits our ability to enjoy nature. Our dominion role has been mismanaged, and our role in the physical order is less nurturing while being more hostile. We are antagonistic (killing off of species), and our lives are filled with drudgery.

Fourth, we have the distinct capacity of knowing God in an intimate way like no other created creature. Yet, many view God as having no interest in their personal lives. Others believe there are many gods, and still others believe God does not exist. Additional examples of a perversion of man's relationship with God are spiritual death, broken fellowship, hampered communication with God, perverted worship, inability to obey, enmity with God while experiencing His wrath and condemnation.

The relational quality of mankind has been so vandalized that we not only have difficulty understanding ourselves, others, and the universe but we even deny the very existence of our Creator! The ultimate effect of sin is eternal separation and rejection by God (Romans 6:23). Mankind's relational dimension is in need of a reconciler.

For further study of the relational dimensions see Appendix F. The scripture references there focus on the four forms of relationships mentioned earlier: man in relationship to God, himself, others, and the creation.

Summary

My intent is not to show that we have six distinct dimensions unrelated to each other, for this would be a distortion of humanity and our abilities. Rather, all six dimensions are interwoven into the fabric of each man and woman. There is both Old and New Testament evidence for the Fall's influence on all aspects of mankind. We are totally depraved and in need of a whole-person Redeemer.

Christians must realize that Christ's liberation has touched each of these dimensions so that man might live a free and abundant life as a relational being created in the image of God.

Notes

[1] I am aware that many individuals understand Romans 7:7-25 as describing the non-Christian or Israel. I believe that verses 7-13 describe the non-Christian while verses 14-25 identifies the Christian. On this see C.E.B. Cranfield, *A Critical and Exegetical Commentary of the Epistle to the Romans* [2 volumes] (ICC Edinburgh: T. & T. Clark, 1975-1979).

[2] Everett F. Harrison, "Romans" in *The Expositor's Bible Commentary, Vol. 10,* Frank E. Gaebelein, General Editor, (Grand Rapids: Zondervan, 1976), p. 82.

[3] D.A. Carson, "Matthew" in *The Expositor's Bible Commentary, Vol. 8,* Frank E. Gaebelein, General Editor, (Grand Rapids: Zondervan, 1984), p. 148.

Review – Section One

The important points of this section are that:

- God made us, humanity, as more than rational beings

- We are spiritual beings comprised of various dimensions:

  ▷ the rational   ▷ the physical

  ▷ the moral   ▷ the volitional

  ▷ the emotional   ▷ the relational

- We must view each complex individual as a whole-person

- Every aspect of every person is touched by sin ("total depravity")

- Every person needs complete healing and salvation from sin

- We cannot heal or save ourselves – we need outside intervention

- Only Jesus Christ can give us the freedom and life we want

The rest of the book focuses upon building and strengthening our lives in the Lord by *abiding in Christ* so that we will be better equipped to help others do the same. We examine what it means to encounter the one true and living God, to be confronted with His holiness, and to live constantly in His presence. We will also scrutinize sin, righteousness and the fruit of the Spirit, and how to help others by providing a safe environment to facilitate further growth.

Throughout the book we explore the fundamental importance of *living by the Great Commandment* –

> You shall love the Lord your God with all your heart, and with all your soul, and with all your mind. (Matthew 22:37)

and how this relates to fulfilling the Great Commission –

> Go therefore and make disciples of all the nations, baptizing them in the name of the Father and the Son and the Holy Spirit, teaching them to observe all that I commanded you. (Matthew 28:19-20a)

At last, we will discover and see that it is really possible to experience now *the life we want in Christ.*

SECTION TWO

The Solution — Light

CHAPTER 3

The Carpenter Begins Rebuilding

The Spirit of the Lord is upon me,
because He anointed me to preach the gospel to the poor.
He has sent me to proclaim release to the captives,
and recovery of sight to the blind,
to set free those who are downtrodden,
to proclaim the favorable year of the Lord.
— Luke 4:18-19 —

The fall of Adam marred all of mankind and every dimension of every person has been infected by Adam's choice. If Jesus came to redeem mankind, his redemption must be for the whole-person. Jesus' ministry focus is outlined in Luke 4:18-19, the passage quoted above. Let's look at some of the ways Jesus ministered to people as whole-persons.

As was Jesus' custom on the Sabbath, He went to the synagogue to worship and pray. A common synagogue activity was to have a reading from the Law and the Prophets. This public reading of God's word was followed by a sermon, often given by a man of the congregation or a rabbi. Jesus was asked to give both the public reading and the sermon. For many this opportunity would have been a very exciting time. He was handed the scroll of Isaiah and He unrolled it to the section He wanted and read it (Isaiah 61:1-2).

I remember returning to my home town having been asked to give the morning sermon. But when the Lutheran pastor found out that I was an evangelical who took the Gospel seriously, I was permitted only to share what my ministry entailed. Nevertheless, I communicated how I share the Gospel and the joy I experience through the process. The response I received from the congregation was in a small part similar to Jesus' reception: a cold and subtle rejection.

Unlike me, however, Jesus was announcing a major portion of his job description: why he was sent by God the Father to earth. You can imagine what the local folk must have thought. Some of them probably remembered watching Jesus play as a child. This man who once played games with their children was now saying this passage in Isaiah was referring to Him! The Jewish rabbis and the general Jewish population understood the passage Jesus read as referring to the Messiah. Jesus boldly and clearly communicated that this passage was written with Him in mind. If Jesus was indeed who He said He was, the people were beholding God in the flesh.

The Spirit Of The Lord Is Upon Me

Jesus announced that he was the possessor of the Holy Spirit. From the very beginning of his ministry, Jesus revealed that he was anointed by his Heavenly Father through the Holy Spirit for an awesome task. Jesus in a sense was commissioned to reach at least four types of people: the poor, the captive, the blind, and the downtrodden. One common element that these kinds of people possess is that they are the unfortunate members of society. Many times they are the first to cry out to God. In essence, Jesus empowered by the Holy Spirit, came to minister to the social outcasts and needy of the land.

Preach The Gospel To The Poor

Jesus announced that he was to proclaim the Gospel to the poor (the Greek word for "gospel" means "good news"). But who are the poor? "Poor" is used in different ways in the New Testament. Luke uses "poor" often throughout his gospel (Luke 6:20, 7:22, 14:13,21, 16:20,22, 18:22, 19:8, and 21:3). In reference to Jesus' proclaiming the Good News to the poor, "Blessed are you who are poor, for yours is the kingdom of God" (Luke 6:20), Luke used poor in the economic and social sense.[1]

Matthew emphasizes the spiritual side of wealth and poverty in Jesus' statement "Blessed are the poor in spirit, for theirs is the kingdom of heaven" (Matthew 5:3). Those who are financially poor are those who lack money, something of great value in this world. Those who are spiritually bankrupt are those who have no relationship with Christ, something of great value in God's kingdom. Those called "poor in spirit" recognize their spiritual poverty apart from Christ, see Christ as the solution to their poor state and realize their spiritual abundance in full under God's reign.

Between these two statements of Jesus, we see the difference between non-Christians, and Christians. The non-believer is spiritually blind and bankrupt apart from knowing Christ and God's rule, while the "poor in spirit," are those who understand that in themselves they are not only spiritually bankrupt but realize their spiritual fullness and riches are in Christ. The "poor in spirit" are blessed for both their right assessment of themselves and of Christ. The non-Christian knows neither. They are in need of a rich relationship with their Creator through Christ. And they are in need of someone who will preach the good news of a healthy relationship with God in light of their deep spiritual poverty.

Proclaim Release To The Captives

The captives are those imprisoned due to some form of debt. Jesus had come to release them from their debtor. This idea of being released from a debt will become clearer when we examine the biblical teaching on the "Year of Jubilee."

According to Luke 3:3, Jesus came preaching a baptism of repentance. The only people who need to repent (a turning from self-reliance to relying on God) are those who have done something wrong and are in need of redirection. The Fall resulted in not only a sinful nature inherited from Adam, but also the heavy guilt and bondage that accompanies it. We are pinned behind the bars of sin and are in need of the key that opens the lock of sinful captivity. Jesus is the only one who possesses this key. He came to set the captives free!

Recovery Of Sight To The Blind

Blindness is the quality or state of lacking light. In Matthew 21:14-16 we see the blind coming to Jesus and receiving their sight. They once walked in physical darkness but through the mighty work of Jesus they received the ability to see, to perceive that which is natural. Yet in Matthew 23:16-26 we learn of a different type of blindness – the inability to perceive that which is supernatural. Jesus rebuked the scribes and Pharisees, men who although they could see physically possessed a fatal case of spiritual blindness. Jesus held them in strict judgment, calling them fools and blind men, for they emphasized that which they could naturally see but were blind to the things of God, things which they were specifically trained to know and understand.

Spiritual blindness can be understood as the inability to perceive the light of the Gospel. Satan has imported an alien culture of blindness, but Jesus has given enlightenment through his Spirit, thereby enabling us to see through the dark culture of the Evil One. Paul informs us that Satan blinds the eyes of non-Christians and indicates that we lived a demonic lifestyle before our salvation (2 Corinthians 4:3-4 and Ephesians 2:1-3). The redemptive work of Christ performs supernatural surgery for our spiritual eyes. As Christians we no longer live in the blinding, binding power of The Evil One – we see and have been set free (1 John 5:19-20).

Jesus indeed healed the physically blind, but more important he came to remove the spiritual blindness instigated, energized, nourished, and encouraged by Satan.

To Set Free Those Who Are Downtrodden

This portion of Jesus' proclamation is taken from Isaiah 58:6. Its interpretation was already combined with the previous phrase "to proclaim release to the captives." This similar idea of freedom was placed here as an emphasis on the need for forgiveness. Forgiveness is the key ingredient for being set free from the bondage of sin.

To Proclaim the Favorable Year Of The Lord

The special year Jesus referred to was the "Year of Jubilee" described in Leviticus 25. There were actually two types of special years to which the Israelites looked forward. The first was the Sabbath Year which was celebrated every seventh year (Deuteronomy 15). Observing the Sabbath Year first began after Israel entered Canaan (Leviticus 25:1-7). Its basic purpose was twofold. First, the land was given a rest. No one was permitted to neither plant any seed nor work the soil in any way. Whatever the soil produced was given to the poor, and all classes of the population lived off the fruit of the land (Exodus 23:11). Second, this seventh year freed all people from previous debts. Lenders were required, by the Sabbath Year law, to close all accounts and forgive any debts owed to them (Deuteronomy 15:2). The Sabbath Year provided an agricultural interlude, food for the poor, and economic release to the people of Israel. A primary reason for this year was to show that it was God's year – this year was "to the Lord" (Leviticus 25:2, 4). Ultimately, the entire universe is God's and is subject to Him and Him only. This celebration was not only liberation from debt and from the hunger of the poor but a reminder of the need to be dependent upon the Creator.

The second special year, the Year of Jubilee, was what Jesus read about from the scroll of Isaiah. According to Leviticus 25:8-9, after seven Sabbath Years had passed, Israel was instructed to sound a trumpet on the tenth day of the seventh month (which was the Day of Atonement). In other words, after forty-nine years had elapsed the Israelites were instructed to celebrate the Year of Jubilee. This fiftieth year jubilee celebration included everything of a Sabbath Year and more. It also required that actual property be returned to the original owner (Leviticus 25:10, 13, and 28).

The Year of Jubilee served as a reminder of the liberation God provided the Israelites from their enslavement under the oppressive rule of the Egyptians (Leviticus 25:42). It communicates that the people of God are not to be enslaved to anyone or anything – they are the people of God! But only through single devotion to the Lord could real freedom from slavery occur. Due to the requirement of this celebration, all land was returned to the family that originally received it as a gift from God when land was divided among the twelve tribes upon entering Canaan. Observing the Year of Jubilee ensured that the original arrangement God made with those who entered the Promised Land would remain in place. The gifts of God are not intended to be lost, stolen, or traded, but are to remain in the hands of the receiver to be used to the glory of the Lord.

The Bible is often filled with shadows or reflections of that which is unseen or is present in heaven. The Year of Jubilee is a type or model of the deliverance of mankind from its slavery to sin. Mankind no longer needs to suffer under the cruel hand of sin's perversion. Just as the land that God gave to the tribes of Israel was restored to its original owners through the Jubilee, all the perverted effects of sin are now being washed away by the Messiah. Mankind and the rest of creation can now be restored and reinstated to their original condition and intent.

Jesus applied the Year of Jubilee to His own ministry. He came to a people who had been sold into slavery because of their own selfishness. He intervened among a people who were blind, poor, and rejected due to the Fall. Not just one part of a person was in need of redemption, but a whole-person redemption was required. The type of restoration Jesus freely offered then and today is not temporal, needing reinstatement but remains throughout eternity.

Today This Scripture Has Been Fulfilled in Your Hearing

We must not overlook Jesus' summary statement: "Today this Scripture has been fulfilled in your hearing" (Luke 4:21). If Jesus did fulfill this portion of Scripture, why do people continue in their bondage? Why do many Christians live a life of entanglement and entrapment to the old ways of a life that they were liberated from on the day of their salvation? Since, according to Jesus, freedom is at their fingertips, what then is wrong?

Notes

[1] Joseph Fitzmyer, *The Gospel According To Luke (I-IX)* (Garden City: Doubleday & Company, Inc., 1981), p. 248.

CHAPTER 4

Knowing the Truth Sets the House Free

Jesus therefore was saying to those Jews who had believed Him,
"If you abide in My word, then you are truly disciples of Mine;
and you shall know the truth, and the truth shall make you free...
Truly, truly, I say to you, everyone who commits sin is the slave of sin...
If therefore the Son shall make you free, you shall be free indeed."
— John 8:31-32, 34, & 36 —

On June 22, 1772, Lord Mansfield, chief justice of the King's Bench, hand-ed down his famous decision that effectively eliminated slavery on the soil of the British Isles. Although slavery had gradually died out in Europe after the introduction of Christianity, it was not officially prohibited, and occa-sionally a slaveowner from overseas would bring slaves with him to Britain. In his celebrated decision, Mansfield held that a slave automatically became a free man by setting foot in Britain. But this decision did not have the slightest effect on slavery in the overseas colonies.

Not until 1811 did William Wilberforce – who had been deeply influ-enced by John Newton, author of "Amazing Grace" – succeed in getting Parliament to ban the slave trade. In 1833 the decision was reached to abol-ish slavery throughout the British Empire over a six year period.[1]

Just as Wilberforce aided in the abolition of slavery by acting upon the decision set down by Lord Mansfield, so each Christian has a similar responsibility to help free non-Christians from their enslavement to sin. Christians need to recognize that free-dom from the bondage of their persistent sins can be realized and experienced through Christ's whole-person redemption.

Writers are told to avoid superlatives. Words such as fabulous, magnificent, and splendid when used too often end up being overstatements and lose their force. Super-latives, such as these, are to be used only when occasions warrant them. Yet when the

Biblical writers wrote of the blessings of God upon his children they used the strongest terms they could find. So great and marvelous are the riches of Christ that the Holy Spirit, the author of Scripture, used the most extravagant language to describe them. As David C. Egner stresses, God's pardon is "abundant" (Isaiah 55:7), his gift of salvation "unspeakable" (2 Corinthians 9:15), and his life "more abundant" (John 10:10).[2] This is the kind of life God desires for all Christians (John 10:10-11). As we experience more and more freedom in Christ, the more we will experience abundant living. The truth that sets us free from sin is the same truth that gives us abundant life.

Steve and Annie Chapman, popular Christian gospel musicians, sing a number of songs related to spiritual growth and family development. Their song "The Secret Place" describes the heart like a "house."[3] One day the Savior began cleaning up the various rooms of his new possession. But when he came to a particular room of the house and asked the man to let him into the room. The man hesitated and said that he did not want Jesus to go into that room because he himself was afraid of that room. As Jesus handed him the key to the locked room, he responded, "You must let me into this room so I can set you free."

Jesus has come to dispense freedom graciously to those who are held in captivity just like the Israelites were set free at the Year of Jubilee who had been enslaved due to their debts. The freedom Jesus offers is not from a temporal debt but from the bonds of sin. For those who abide in Christ, the bondage and weight of sin is lifted and freedom results. The abundant life Jesus spoke of (John 10) is not experienced by simply a rational approach to Scripture but entails an intimate relationship with God.

Throughout the New Testament truth is closely associated with Christ. Jesus described himself as "the way, the truth, and the life" (John 14:6). As we maintain an intimate relationship with Christ, who is the living truth, we experience freedom. This sounds great, but how can we maintain an intimate relationship with Christ practically? As we consider this question we must keep in mind that freedom from sin is linked to truth and that Jesus is the truth.

Freedom in the Rational Dimension

At the supper table my wife has often asked "Who are you talking to?," as she observes my lips moving and my head nodding. We all experience conversations within our minds.[4] Frequently, however, there are ideas, comments, and responses that flash through our minds that we do not know directly where they come from. At the same time many of these thoughts are not true. Problems arise when we believe and act upon such falsehoods. A large portion of our nurture and development in the non-rational dimensions of our being is achieved in setting an atmosphere where wrong beliefs, attitudes, and values can be identified and replaced by truth. Yet we must not be satisfied with an education that is called Christian when the filling of the rational dimension is seen as the primary and the only necessary dimension of our humanity that needs to be changed.

Many of us are well aware that often our knowledge far exceeds our lifestyles. There is a great chasm between what we know in our minds as truth and what we experience as truth in our lives. Christianity is a lifestyle built upon practicing and obeying the truths of Scripture as we grow in intimacy and trust with our heavenly Father. The Great Commission (Matthew 28:20) speaks of teaching people to obey, not just filling their heads with facts. Obedience assumes practice and is in no way equivalent to mental acknowledgment or agreement.

Remember the song "It is Finished" mentioned in the introduction of this book? Two-thirds of the way through the song the singer mentions that even though the battle had been won he was not aware of it. He was living in such a way that the battle was still going on. Even though as Christians we already stand before God free and victorious in Christ, most of us live in practical bondage to some form of sin (Romans 7:15). We must learn how to practically apply the truth of freedom from any sin to our everyday experience. While we need to understand accurately the biblical truths of our position and freedom in Christ, at the same time we must experience in our lives what we give intellectual assent to. Both positionally and practically the only means of freedom is in Christ (Romans 8:1-15).

A primary work of the Holy Spirit is to enlighten us with an understanding of the Scriptures. Years ago, when I was packing my bags for college, I placed my Bible in my suitcase. Why? I'm not sure other than I thought it would look good on my desk. In my first two years of college I picked up the Bible one time and while reading it concluded that I had no idea what it was talking about. In my junior year at Pennsylvania State University, after I became a Christian, the Bible became alive! Why? It was because the Holy Spirit opened my mind to understand the truths of God. Now as the Spirit enables me to understand correctly and energizes me to obey, I experience freedom in my life as I put into practice the truths that I have been enabled to understand. My old beliefs, attitudes, and values are in the process of being replaced with the truths of God.

An example of beliefs, attitudes, and values being manifested through one's life is seen in Daniel 4. There we find the story of Nebuchadnezzar, king of Babylon, becoming like an animal as judgment and a lesson from God. Nebuchadnezzar arrogantly believed that he had made himself great as the sovereign of Babylon. But God, the Most High, decided that Nebuchadnezzar would have his mind changed from that of a man to that of a beast for time until he recognized that God "is the ruler over the realm of mankind, and bestows it on whomever He wishes" (4:25). After Nebuchadnezzar's experience of insanity and of living, eating, and acting like an animal, his reason returned to him. Note the remarkable change that took place. Nebuchadnezzar humbled himself and praised, exalted, and honored the King of heaven. Why? Because his reason was returned to him and his thinking had changed as he acknowledged God as the Most High and started to live according to God's ways. His new beliefs directly influenced his whole being as reflected in every area of his life. This is an example of how the various dimensions of our humanity have their roots in the rational dimension. The rational dimension is the door to our attitudes, values, and beliefs, and it is expressed and seen through the various windows of our house. While our sinfulness applies to the whole-person, so does Christ's redemption: truth has been given to us to understand and to live.

Freedom in the Physical Dimension

Matthew 9 describes Jesus' healing a woman who suffered from a twelve-year hemorrhage, giving sight to two blind men, raising a young girl from the dead, healing a demon-possessed man, and that Jesus was going about healing every kind of disease and sickness. This shows that a very real part of Christ's ministry pertains to the physical liberation of man from diseases, illness, and even death. But Jesus knows that our primary need is liberation from the enslaving power of sin which causes our physical difficulties. Even though Jesus had his vision set continually on the cross, he spent valuable time ministering to the physical needs of people for at least two reasons: 1) mankind is made in the image of God and was not originally designed to live with a faulty and marred physical body, and 2) the healing of people's physical afflictions often provided an opportunity to minister to their deeper spiritual needs and their problem of sin.

The value of healing and easing the physical pains of life is emphasized throughout the Bible. It is necessary for the believer to care for and develop his body, which is the temple of God. Like Elijah, sometimes all we need is sleep and food to aid the body (1 Kings 19:5-9), but then there are times when radical medical intervention is warranted.

I have been very thankful to the Lord for the wisdom and knowledge he has revealed to humanity through medical research as both my parents have greatly benefited from surgery and the use of many medications. Even though we do not possess the ability to heal every type of disease and illness, we do have the capacity to be involved in the healing process. The ability to help anyone physically through the means of medical technology has only come from the gracious hand of our Creator and Father. Thus, care for and nurture of the human body is not only an expression of spirituality, but it is also a legitimate aspect and means of discipleship (but it is not enough in and of itself). Just as Jesus did what was within his ability to help and to heal others, so we, as part of our ministry, can employ aid for others' physical needs with medicine, food, clothing, shelter, etc. Activities such as these can also be done in partnership with and in the name of evangelism. This kind of ministry may lead to the presentation of a fuller understanding of the liberation of mankind by Christ and lead to redemption.

There may be many who recognize the value of helping individuals with their physical needs simply because they themselves have experienced similar assistance. But there is a far more important reason to help with individual physical needs.

As we follow the path of Moses and the Israelites out of Egypt, we discover that the tabernacle was a vital part of their lives. Great care was given to the construction and upkeep of this structure for it often housed the very presence of God Almighty (Exodus 35-38). It should come as no surprise that the time spent in the construction and the economic cost of the tabernacle was great.

As we study the era of David and his son Solomon, we also see that a major emphasis was placed on the temple of God. King David was provoked to action when he contemplated that he himself dwelt in a house of cedar, but the ark of God dwelt in a tent (2 Samuel 7:2)! David was not permitted to construct the temple for God; however, he was permitted to collect the materials and money necessary for the temple's construction. In addition, he purchased the plot of land where the temple was to be erected (1 Chronicles 22:8, 3:2; 2 Samuel 24:18-25). 1 Kings 6-8 shows the great detail and care concerning the building of the temple of God. It was a sacred place to be respected, honored, and properly cared for.

Throughout Old Testament times and into the New Testament era, the temple of God was always reverenced by God's people. Even Jesus honored it by calling it the house of God (John. 2:16). But the honor that Jesus attributed to the temple was only due to the fact that God made his dwelling with mankind there. Also, the things which the temple contained were holy because they were sanctified by the God who dwelt within (Matthew 23:17, 21). Knowing its true significance is what moved Jesus to cleanse the temple from the sacrilegious activities which were taking place in it during the Passover (John. 2:13-17).

But what of the temple today? Where does God reside? He resides not in a traveling tabernacle made from animal skins nor does he take up residence in a temple made by human hands. God resides within the believer in the person of the Holy Spirit (1 Corinthians 3:16). Just as the Israelites in Moses' time, as the Israelites in the times of David and Solomon, and as Jesus took care of God's dwelling places (the tabernacle, the temple, and the synagogue), then we should give no less attention to care for the temple of the Holy Spirit – our bodies. Just as Jesus drove the unwanted money changers from the temple of God, He also liberated the Christian's body from the unwanted visitor of eternal death: "'Oh, death where is your sting'" (1 Corinthians 15:55)? Even though we may undergo physical death, its stinger has been removed: eternal death no longer exists for the Christian! Our physical bodies will be resurrected and glorified because of the liberating work of Christ.

While living on earth within our sin marred physical bodies, Jesus' freedom means a radical cleansing of the perverted use and activity of his temple (John 2:13-17). The effects of Adam's decision in the Garden long ago still linger and manifest themselves in the great needs evident in the physical domain. One day the body will be resurrected to a glorious state, but until that time we must view and minister to the body as an integral part of what it means to be both human and Christian.

Freedom in the Moral Dimension

Confusion can be a frequent companion of those who are striving for absolutes to embrace. Yet freedom to do whatever you want, regardless of absolutes, is popular today. This attitude is very similar to that mentioned in Judges 17:6: "every man did what was right in his own eyes." Notice that each individual was his own source of right and wrong. To be sure, contemporary thought is no different: we simply say right and wrong are relative. The true sense of morality has to do with 'oughtness' (what ought to be) and requires a standard. But the society we live in defines morality not by 'ought' but by 'is'. Whatever we do, whatever turns us on, whatever feels good, these fashion the ethical grid!

Our situation is very similar to the one described in Judges 17:6: "In those days there was no king in Israel; every man did what was right in his own eyes." The king was looked to as the authority that set and enforced the laws of the land for the good of the people. When no king existed, each individual became independent and took upon himself kingship by judging rightness and wrongness. The individual no longer functioned as a servant depending upon the king for direction, but became a self-serving king. He set himself on the throne as a rebel king and determined what ought to be.

This is a far cry from how God defines and measures morality. The Ten Commandments give us the 'ought' which governs the 'is'. Our society works in reverse and says that the 'ought' is determined by the 'is'. Human morality is relativistic and man-centered; God's morality is absolute and God-centered. The Christian's oughtness, his morality, is based on the Ten Commandments and was summarized by Jesus. When asked by a lawyer what the greatest commandment in the Law was, Jesus responded:

> You shall love the Lord your God with all your heart, and with all your soul, and with all you mind." This is the great and foremost commandment. And a second is like it, "You shall love your neighbor as yourself." On these two commandments depend the whole Law and the Prophets. (Matthew 22:37-40)

Jesus' response to the lawyer's inquiry was whole-person. Obedience to these commandments requires a total response from us. Jesus indicates that love for Him is manifested in loving obedience (John 14:21). This action has to be based upon God's morality, God's word. The Bible is the Christian's moral code book: there is no other. God does not tolerate rivals! Our morals, the standards by which we live, are an indication of his Lordship or our lack of such commitment. We are not surprised that today's society has composed its own national and individual standards, for its moral dimension is depraved.

Jesus often referred to the Law of Moses and to the Prophets, yet we discover that Jesus set an even higher standard. We find that those who attempted to keep the law of God placed a strong emphasis on the external activities of life. But Jesus underscored that God's Law requires going beyond the mere external adherence to an internalizing of its truth. For while the Law says, "You shall not commit adultery," Jesus emphasized that even to entertain and dwell on thoughts or fantasies of sexual activities with anyone other than one's God-given mate is adultery. This is the true heart and meaning of the commandment "You shall not commit adultery." Jesus revealed that God is not only interested in what we do externally with our bodies, but also with our thoughts and intentions.[5] Jesus knew that if we do not possess victory in our minds, we will never experience victory in our normal everyday behaviors. We cannot and will never be able to do so apart from the liberating work of Christ. Through Jesus we can experience the depth and breadth of moral freedom required by our heavenly

Father. Jesus is the one who washes away the old standards of right and wrong designed by a depraved and self-centered mind. This cleansing of our moral dimension comes through the Word of God.

John the Apostle testified that Jesus is the Word and John the Baptist declared that Jesus is the lamb of God who takes away the sins of the world (John 1:1 and 29). Since it is truth that sets us free, then the only one who can free us from the moral dilemmas of mankind is Jesus. When Jesus occupies the throne of our lives and rules supreme, then we experience moral freedom. The standards of the king become those of his servants because He reigns and not we ourselves. Instead of experiencing bondage to sin, by declaring our independence in Christ we experience freedom by submitting to and acknowledging our dependence on King Jesus.

Freedom in the Volitional Dimension

A vital dimension of our humanity is choice. Choosing becomes particularly important when we realize that we live in a society that encourages us to not take responsibility for our actions but to blame the consequences of our choices on others, our past, or something else beyond our control. But we must realize that there is a great difference between "I can't" and "I won't." "I can't" means that what has been requested is beyond my ability and, therefore, I am not able. "I won't" indicates ability, that I have a choice and have decided to choose negatively.

But what of our wills when we consider the effects of sin? We discovered earlier that man's volitional dimension has been sabotaged by sin and therefore our ability to choose that which is pleasing to God has been hindered. Adam made many choices in the garden. He was given the responsibility to name all the animals of the earth – that's a lot of decisions! Before the fall, Adam's will had no predisposition to sin. There were no sinful tendencies within Adam influencing him to do evil. He was free to choose apart from having an inclination toward sin. But when Adam chose to sin, the results left every human with an overwhelming bent towards evil. So strong is this predisposition we are told in the Bible that we are unable to choose to do good even if we want to.

How can anyone choose Christ (a good choice pleasing to God) if this evil influence is overwhelming and consuming? Part of the Holy Spirit's role is to enable the non-Christian to freely choose Christ. Without the Holy Spirit's regenerational work there exists no possible chance for a non-Christian to accept Christ. Through the Holy Spirit's work, the non-Christian is freed and enabled to choose Christ. The Holy

Spirit's work in non-Christian's lives is not easily seen, but nonetheless the Spirit is working in them convicting of sin, righteousness, and judgment.

The Holy Spirit actually enters a person's life at the time of conversion. God's Spirit begins to reside permanently in the Christian's life – convicting, teaching, enlightening, etc., – all to the glory of God. With non-Christians, while the Holy Spirit does not reside within them, the Spirit's work in their lives can be described as working from the outside to the inside while for the Christian the work is from the inside out.[6] By this I mean that the Holy Spirit does not take up residence within a non-Christian but rather works, usually unaware to the non-Christian, by drawing the person to Christ and then giving the person the ability to choose to follow Christ.[7] As we seek to minister to others and share the gospel of Christ, we must pray for discernment to discover how the Holy Spirit is and has already been working in their lives.

Paul once wrote that he wrestled with doing what he really did not want to do even though he had the desire to do what is right, "but I cannot carry it out" (Romans 7:18). Before an individual chooses to follow Christ he cannot please God, but once an individual chooses to follow Christ the Spirit enables him to choose to do what God wants if the believer lives by faith (Galatians 2:20). In other words, a non-Christian possesses no ability or desire to please God. The Holy Spirit, however, can free a non-Christian's will so that he can choose Christ. Once a person becomes a Christian he is in the state that Paul wrote of: the wishing or desiring to do good is present but he cannot carry it out. He is a Christian and is in Christ positionally. The ability to choose to please God is found in Christ Jesus (Romans 8:1-15). Once a Christian is in Christ he not only has the desire to please God but he can choose to please God by abiding in Christ practically. The chart below outlines and summarizes these various states.

Individual	Wishing To Do Good	Doing Good	Pleasing To God
Non-Christian (Romans 3:10-18)	No	No	No
Christian (Romans 7:14-25) *Positional Abiding*	Yes	No	No

Individual	Wishing To Do Good	Doing Good	Pleasing To God
Christian **(Romans 8:1-15)** *Positional and* *Practical Abiding*	Yes	Yes	Yes

Paul's command for us to "put on the new self, which in the likeness of God has been created in righteousness and holiness of the truth" (Ephesians 4:24) integrated with his teaching in Romans 7-8 helps to explain how abiding in the practical sense functions.

The renewing of our minds is not a renovation or evolution of the mind, but a *re-creation,* the making of a "new self." Christians are a new species, humans who have "become partakers of the divine nature" (2 Peter 1:4). The term "righteousness" (or right living) is usually used in regard to our fellowman. This is clearly seen in the Ten Commandments in commands five through ten (Exodus 20:12-17). "Holiness" is to be understood as something or someone set apart for God's use and as being pure or purified vessels relating to our Creator. This idea is reflected in commands one through four of the Ten Commandments (Exodus 20:3-11).

The new self is one of holiness and righteousness and no sin can result from this divine nature. Understanding the new self clarifies why Paul places the source of sin outside the new self (Romans 6-7). Furthermore, Paul commands us to not let sin reign in our mortal bodies and that we should not continue presenting the members of our bodies to sin (Romans 6:12-13). Understanding this we see why Paul places the source of the believer's sin in the body. Thus he proclaims:

> So now, no longer am I the one doing it, but sin which indwells me. For I know that nothing good dwells in me, that is, in my flesh; for the wishing is present in me, but the doing of the good is not. For the good that I wish, I do not do, but I practice the very evil that I do not wish. But if I am doing the very thing I do not wish, I am no longer the one doing it, but sin which dwells in me. I find then the principle that evil is present in me, the one who wishes to do good (Romans 7:17-21).

Paul goes on to clearly point to our problem: "I see a different law in the members of my body, waging war against the law of my mind, and making me prisoner of the law of sin which is in my members" (Romans 7:24). Once Paul explains the problem he then makes his appeal: "Wretched man that I am! Who will set me free from the body of this death?" (Romans 7:25). Having step-by-step explained our dual state of having a renewed mind and a corrupted flesh, followed by the problem of the conflict between these two, Paul strategically leads us to the solution: "For the law of the Spirit of life in Christ Jesus has set you free from the law of sin and of death" (Romans 8:2). Paul refers us to the practical abiding relationship with Christ. Acknowledging Christ moment-by-moment will supernaturally result in doing the things I want to do. This indeed is the life I want in Christ.

Three Aspects of Abiding in Christ

Three important distinctions need to be made in regard to abiding. First, every Christian is in Christ positionally. This happens at rebirth and can never change. Second, Christians have been delivered from the guilt and judgment of sin but not automatically from its power. Third, only when we practically abide in Christ are we enabled to do what the Spirit wants us to do. Chapters six and seven specifically focus upon abiding in Christ in the practical sense.

As an educator, I am very interested in how people grow. I recognize that a major portion of my role is to plant and water and that God is the one who causes people to grow. How God causes people to grow in light of their free will is a mystery to me. I am content to live within the limits of my finiteness while I serve God and others the best I know how, and to be content with what God does regardless of my lack of complete understanding. My desire is that you will be free to do the same.

The Christian must be willing to do what is right before the power is given to do righteousness. Paul teaches us this very important truth in Colossians 3:12-14:

> And so, as those who have been chosen of God, holy and beloved, put on a heart of compassion, kindness, humility, gentleness and patience; bearing with one another, and forgiving each other, whoever has a complaint against anyone; just as the Lord forgave you, so also should you. And beyond all these things put on love, which is the perfect bond of unity.

Paul commands the believer to *put on* a heart of compassion, kindness, etc. . . . and to *put on* love. Putting on is not an emotion; it is an act of the will. If an individual is unwilling, not unable, to set his mind on the things above (Colossians 3:2), further growth is impossible. Vital to Christian development is that we embrace the reality that we are free to choose, for without this recognition growth stagnates. Freedom is a delightful fruit to enjoy as we experience the liberation Christ has given. We are not in bondage to Satan, sin, emotions, or others. We are free *in Christ!* The ability to choose must become a living reality for our volitional dimension to operate in a way that is pleasing to God (1 Corinthians 10:13). We have the ability to choose and are accountable for what we choose (Romans 14:12).

Genuine, biblical freedom gives us the ability to do what we were designed to do and enables us to be who we were designed to be. It is not the "freedom" to do what we want to do. Design refers to what God originally created us to do (i.e., to love God and our neighbors). In a very direct sense, our original design defines and delineates what we ought to do. Oughtness has to do with ethics and for the Christian ethics have an absolute moral standard: God. Thus, moral absolutes are not composed of personal desires, decrees, or goals but only those from God above. Even as Paul exhorts, "Set your mind on the things from above, not on things that are on earth" (Colossians 3:2). Here a number of human dimensions are working together underscoring the truth that no one dimension ever functions wholly apart from interaction with the others. The moral (standard) always interacts with the rational (attitudes, values, and beliefs) and the volitional (will) dimensions of ones humanity.

Freedom of choice always operates in connection with and in the shadow of accountability to the absolute standard of God. As a result, our choices and actions always have consequences closely tied to them. We could say that our freedom of choice is actually the responsibility to choose and act wisely in accordance to the will of God: freedom is responsibility.

The volitional dimension is best employed by saying "No" to both immoral things as well as to many good things. Saying no to the bad is easily recognized as valid when keeping biblical commands in mind. Saying no to some good things, such as teaching another Sunday school class, being on another committee, attending another dinner engagement, etc., while difficult may be the best choice in light of other priorities one may have. You may be surprised to discover that to say no to a ministry opportunity may be pleasing to God. Suffice it for now to say that we will discuss in a later chapter that our highest priority is the Great Commandment not the Great Commission.

Volitional freedom is not the ability to do what we want to *do* but be what we were designed to *be.* Here we see how the volitional and moral dimensions work hand-in-hand. We are designed to function as a whole-person. The door and windows are networked together by God's design.

In Psalm 119:59-60 the writer wrote that he considered (thought about or reflected upon) his ways and then chose to obey the law of God. Christians have been freed to choose and have been given the Bible which provides the boundaries for our choices. This is not to suggest that if we are having a repeated problem with a particular sin or areas of sin that all we need to do is simply choose and the problem is over. The point here is that our ability to choose comes from being in Christ.

Freedom in the Emotional Dimension

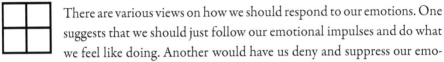 There are various views on how we should respond to our emotions. One suggests that we should just follow our emotional impulses and do what we feel like doing. Another would have us deny and suppress our emotions and treat them as a curse. Such views pervert the truth and must be rejected. Emotions are a gift from God, an essential part of being human, and they must be properly understood and used for his kingdom. We are emotional beings and need to understand how our rational and volitional dimensions influence our emotional states. Since our rational and volitional states can be in error, our emotional states may also need correction. We need to remember that our emotional dimension has been marred by sin, and, therefore, that we are capable of handling and expressing our emotions in sinful ways.

Fear and anxiety are two common emotions that may be direct results of our sinful natures. Did fear and anxiety exist in the Garden of Eden before the fall of man? In Isaiah 41:10 we are commanded not to fear. But this is more than just a recommendation not to fear, for Isaiah tells us why we should not fear: God is with us. In Philippians 4:6-7 we are told that we should not worry or be anxious regarding anything. Instead when tempted to worry we are to take our concerns to God "by prayer and supplication with thanksgiving... and the peace of God which surpasses all comprehension, shall guard your hearts and your minds in Christ Jesus." Both of these passages are addressed to believers. Individuals designed to have fellowship with God but those who do not know Him naturally have fear and anxiety. Unfortunately, fear and anxiety are also common among many Christians. Where does such fear come from?

In Genesis 3 we find Adam and Eve, who were created to enjoy the presence of God and to walk in step with him, suddenly afraid of God's presence and they attempt to hide from him. Our sin and guilt causes us to fear and to run from God, when, in fact, he is the only one who can help us! Our Lord is the one who says, "Do not fear for I am with you; do not anxiously look about you, for I am your God . . . ." (Isaiah 41:10). We, like the non-Christian, experience what Adam and Eve encountered for the first time in the garden.

For many of us it is difficult to honestly admit or even accept our emotional states. Recently while I was yelling at one of my children, my wife asked me why I was angry. I responded, "I'm not angry!" If we cannot admit or accept our emotional states and manage them in a godly way, we will suffer under the bondage of sin which can lead to the bondage of bitterness, depression, and other emotionally- related states. When we honestly come to grips with the reality of the sinful aspects of our emotional dimension, we are then on the road to freedom and abundant living. The Christian, through abiding in Christ, has all the necessary ingredients to respond in godly ways that bring pleasure to our Lord and peace to us.

Freedom in the Relational Dimension

Since we are created in the image of a triune God, it should come as no surprise that we have a relational dimension. We see the three-fold Godhead interacting and relating in perfect unity and harmony. This is the ideal relational model for mankind. Through Christ's incarnation, we see his perfect example of relating to the Father and to the Holy Spirit. While unity does not mean uniformity, there exists great unity in the midst of diverse responsibility within the Trinity.

We are relational beings, a fact demonstrated in at least four different yet overlapping relationships. They are: 1) in relationship with God, 2) in relationship with yourself, 3) in relationship with others; and 4) in relationship with creation. But relational depravity is seen in Genesis 3 with Adam and Eve's relationship with God and each other at the Fall. Rather than seeking companionship with the Lord, they attempted to hide from him. Clearly, they did not want him to know they had disobeyed him. Once 'found' by the God who seeks ("Where are you?"), they invent the blame game (see Genesis 3:9-12): And the man said, "The woman whom Thou gavest to be with me, she gave me from the tree, and I ate." Then the Lord God said to the woman, "What is this you have done?" And the woman said, "The serpent deceived me, and I ate."

Adam not only blames Eve ("she gave me from the tree"), he also lays blame at God's feet ("The woman whom Thou gavest to be with me"). Eve does Adam one better by compressing blame on the serpent with a moral/psychological excuse ("the serpent deceived me"). Even today, we still have people trying to hide from God and playing the blame game.

John Stott shows that as a consequence of sin we are 1) alienated from God, 2) in bondage to our self, and 3) in conflict with others. We could add to his list that we are 4) poor stewards of creation.[8] Christ came to liberate us so that we may have a perfect relationship with the triune God, ourselves, our neighbors, and God's marvelous creation.

Comparing ourselves to one another is a problem we all seem to share. As a result of our comparisons, we develop at least one of the following attitudes: 1) arrogance, the "I'm better than you are and, therefore, I am more important" attitude; or 2) inadequacy, the "They are better than I am and, therefore, they must be more important than I am" attitude. Each of these perspectives is sinful and must be avoided. It is understandable that non-Christians compare themselves to others, but the real mystery is why we Christians do it.

Even Peter had a problem with comparison. After receiving a task from Jesus, Peter asked, "Lord, and what about this man?" Too often we are comparing ourselves to others and thinking the same thing: "Well, what about them?" How do we match up? Jesus' response to us is the same as it was to Peter: ". . .what is that to you? You follow Me!" (John 21:20-22). Remember Paul's counsel?

> I urge you therefore, brethren, by the mercies of God, to present your bodies a living and holy sacrifice, acceptable to God, which is your spiritual service of worship. And do not be conformed to this world, but be transformed by the renewing of your mind, that you may prove what the will of God is, that which is good and acceptable and perfect. For through the grace given to me I say to every man among you not to think more highly of himself than he ought to think; but to think so as to have sound judgment, as God has allotted to each a measure of faith. (Romans 12:1-3)

One conviction (belief) that has really helped me is that I am the most gifted, talented, and qualified person to do what God has called me to do. According to Ephesians 2:10, God has already created good works for me to walk in. Since God has *already* created good works for me to do, it seems reasonable that he has already equipped or will equip me to walk in them. Do you see the freedom, and confidence, this gives me? I do not have to compare myself with or compete with you or anyone else. God already has things for *each* of us to do, and as we keep our eyes on him (not on ourselves or others) he will lead us to what he has made for us to do.

We do not have to compare and worry about competing with others. We need to realize that all the gifts, talents, and abilities we possess have been given to us to glorify God, and that if we need additional talents or resources God will give them to us. When we accept and grasp the truth of God's word, the result is personal peace and freedom and we end up working together against the evil one rather than being divided and being used as his pawns.

Only as we properly understand our God can we properly understand our relational capacities. Only as we abide in his presence and comprehend the truth of his Word can we come to experience a sane estimate of ourselves and be properly equipped to relate to and respond in godly ways to others and to our environment (creation). Jesus said that we will be known as his disciples by our love for one another (John 13:35). Our relationships with those in the unbelieving world as well as those in the family of God have the highest importance in the perspective of God.

The spark to proper relationships is ignited through the liberating flame of the redemptive work of Jesus Christ. Thus, to live an abundant life, to be fully human, each person needs to be led to the Master and taught how to abide in him. Samuel Shoemaker, a Christian leader of the 1950's, carved the following words in the stone of the Frick Fine Arts Building at the University of Pittsburgh:

> Our universities are places of learning which will prove to be blind guides unless they lead those insecure seeking young people, not alone to knowledge and the beginning of wisdom but to the source of all wisdom. That which needs to be known most is how to live and how to live with others.

The Christian's relational responsibility can be further understood by considering the following passage taken from The Lausanne Covenant, International Congress on World Evangelization, Lausanne, Switzerland, July 1974:

> We affirm that God is both the Creator and the Judge of all men. We therefore should share his concern for justice and reconciliation throughout human society and for the liberation of men from every kind of oppression. Because mankind is made in the image of God, every person, regardless of race, religion, color, culture, class, sex or age, has an intrinsic dignity be-

cause of which he should be respected and served, not exploited. Here too we express penitence both for our neglect and for having sometimes regarded evangelism and relational concern as mutually exclusive. Although reconciliation with man is not reconciliation with God, nor is relational action evangelism, nor is political liberation salvation, nevertheless we affirm that evangelism and relational political involvement are both part of our Christian duty. For both are necessary expressions of our doctrines of God and man, our love for our neighbor and our obedience to Jesus Christ. The message of salvation implies also a message of judgment upon every form of alienation, oppression and discrimination, and we should not be afraid to denounce evil and injustice wherever they exist. When people receive Christ they are born again into his kingdom and must seek not only to exhibit but also to spread its righteousness in the midst of an unrighteous world. The salvation we claim should be transforming us in the totality of our personal and relational responsibilities. Faith without works is dead (Acts 17:26,31; Genesis 18:25; Isaiah 1:17; Psalm 45:7; Genesis 1:26,27; James 3:9; Leviticus 19:18; Luke 6:27,35; James 2:14-26; John 3:3-5; Matthew 5:20; 6:33; 2 Corinthians 3:18; James 2:20).[9]

Truth, Freedom, and Discipleship

Understanding discipleship in and through each of the six dimensions of our humanity provides a whole-person approach to personal growth and for the discipling of others. If one of the dimensions of our lives consumes us and becomes the primary focus of our lives, then emptiness and shallowness will occur. We must never isolate or stress one dimension over the others, but see each as an interwoven thread in the entire fabric of our humanness. There may be brief times when we must focus on one or two of these dimensions (e.g., the physical when we are sick, the emotional when we are happy or sad, the moral when we are called to make ethical decisions, etc.), but we must always keep the others in mind and guard against neglecting them.

Without understanding the necessity of a deep and abiding relationship with Christ and the need for whole-person development we will remain in or return to sin's bondage. An unshackled, highly illuminated house is the fullest expression of what it means to be human.

Jesus is the truth and "it was for freedom that Christ set us free" (Galatians 5:1). But this freedom is not given to us to love self but to love and serve God and others

(Galatians 5:13-14). The central purpose of the incarnation was to set people free from the oppression and penalty of sin. Derek Tidball expresses it well:

> Freedom was one of Paul's great themes (Romans 8:1-17; Galatians 5:1) and it was amply suited to his world. Many a slave longed for freedom from his human master and worked hard to earn it. Christ's work was a work of manumission [freedom from slavery] given to men who could not possibly earn it. When a man had been set free he would usually adopt the status of his former master. The Christian convert too received a new status; the status of being Christ's man (2 Corinthians 5:17). The Christian's freedom, however, is not a freedom which allows him to enjoy a selfish independence. It is curiously enough a freedom which bounds him in a new form of slavery; a slavery to God (Romans 6:15-23). This slavery paradoxically was a perfect form of liberty. In it man learned to serve his Lord (Romans 12:11; 4:18; Colossians 3:24) and his fellow Christians (Galatians 5:13), not because he was forced to but out of voluntary submission. The crux of this paradox of slavery and freedom lay, for the Christian, in the fact that his master, the Lord of all, had himself voluntarily become a slave and taken upon himself the full consequences of being a slave to the extent of accepting the death penalty (Philippians 2:1-11). In this way not only was his lordship confirmed but he became an example to all believers.[10]

The core of discipleship is to help people discover true freedom and to facilitate an atmosphere conducive to a liberated lifestyle in Christ. Again, this freedom is not the ability to do what we want to do, but the responsibility to be and do who and what we are designed to be and do (Luke 1:74,75; Romans 6:16-18, 20). We bring glory to God not only by exercising our spiritual gifts, but by living righteously as we become all of what he created us to be: "Whether, then, you eat or drink or whatever you do, do all to the glory of God" (1 Corinthians 10:31). Discipleship involves our whole-person and whatever we do should be done out of gratitude towards our heavenly Father.

Truth and light work very well together. As we understand the truth of the gospel, we suddenly see through the darkness and we, in a very real sense, become more like Christ. The principle that we become like the one's we live around is easily seen in the Christian who spends more and more time abiding in and experiencing the presence of Christ. This is a foundational truth underlying discipleship. When we are abiding in Christ, we cannot help but influence those around us. It comes as no surprise that experiencing the truth characterizes the disciple of Christ, for Christ is truth. The disciple of Christ is expected to both practice (the Great Commandment) and use that truth to further the kingdom of God (the Great Commission).

There exists a sharp contrast between a profession of faith and one that is lived out. This tension is inconsistent with abiding in Christ: "If we say that we have fellowship with Him and yet walk in darkness, we lie and do not practice the truth" (1 John 1:6). The truth we discover in Christ is not to be confused with the truth found in the social sciences. Even though truth discovered through the social sciences has its source in Christ, the truth spoken of in the Gospel of John is saving truth. It is faith in Christ that saves us from our sin rather than just from error and ignorance. This relates back to what Jesus said of his ministry: he came to release the captives (Luke 4:18). The sad and frightening thing is that people do not usually realize that they are in bondage, but rather rest in the false security of lust, avarice, and power.

Summary

There are four consecutive, progressively-related points Jesus makes in defining freedom (John 8:31-32):

   i)   If you abide in My word,
   ii)   then you are truly disciples of Mine;
   iii)   and you shall know the truth,
   iv)   and the truth shall make you free.

But free from what? Free for-what? Christian liberty has both positive and negative sides. The negative consists of liberation from bondage to the rules and standards of the world (Galatians 4:8, 9; 5:1; Colossians 2:20-22), from bondage to sin and its power (Romans 6:14,18), from bondage of the fear and power of death (Hebrews 2:14-15; 1 Corinthians 15:54-57), from Satan's power (Acts 26:18; Colossians 1:13; Hebrews 2:14,15), and from God's wrath (Isaiah 42:7; 60:1; Romans 8:1). The positive consists of liberation to be free, to be who and what we are created to be, free to do the will of God, free to live in righteousness, and free to enjoy eternal life in Christ Jesus! (Romans 6:16-23; 1 Corinthians 7:22).

Notes

[1] Paul Lee Tan, Encyclopedia of 7700 Illustrations (Rockville, MD: Assurance Publications, 1979), p. 461.

[2] Ibid., p. 517.

[3] Paul Steven Chapman, (Careers-BMG Music Publishing, Inc., 1981). The standard treatment of this idea is found in the booklet *My Heart, Christ's Home* (New Expanded Edition) by Robert Boyd Munger (Downers Grove: InterVarsity Press, 1986. Bob Bennett also has very similar ideas in his song "You're Welcome Here," Written by Bob Bennett, © 1978 Maranatha! Music (admin. by the Copyright Company, Nashville, TN) All rights reserved. International Copyright Secured. Used by permission.

Lord, I hear you knocking

You've been knocking at the door

How long have you been waiting?

Seems I never really heard you before

I've kind of let the place go

I'm ashamed of what you'll find

But you can make yourself at home

If you're sure that you don't mind

Chorus

'Cause when I cry, the roof leaks,

And when the wind blows, the walls are weak

But a house is known by the company it keeps

And I feel better now that you're near

And I want to make it clear

Jesus, from now on, you're always welcome here

There are dark rooms deep inside me

Where your light has never shown

And I tried to hide inside them

But I guess you've always known

That one day you would call me

And I'd awaken from my sleep

And you'd take me just the way I am

And you'd promise that you'd keep me

Chorus

[4] See David Stoop, *Self-Talk: Key to Personal Growth, Second Edition*-(Grand Rapids: Fleming H. Revell, 1996) for an excellent in-depth treatment of this subject. For those who work with others, see H. Norman Wright, Self-Talk, Imagery, and Prayer in Counseling, Resources for Christian Counseling, #3 (Dallas: Word, Inc., 1986).

[5] See Matthew 5-7, the Sermon on the Mount, which contains other examples of Jesus' understanding of the Law.

[6] See Larry Crabb, *Inside Out* (Colorado Springs: NavPress, 1988) on this idea.

[7] I realize that there are a number of highly debated issues between those who embrace either a Calvinistic or Arminian view of salvation. I in no way want to make light of either view, but my presentation serves in my mind to best reconcile what the Scriptures teach about salvation. My prayer is that if you disagree with me here, do not allow this difference to inhibit the main issues of this book. Regardless of your views on how one obtains salvation, the main issues of this book (whole-person development and abiding in Christ) will still be helpful. Whether you tend to be of the Calvinist or of the Arminian persuasion,

the Holy Spirit is still ministering among the lost.

[8]John R.W. Stott has an excellent treatment of "The Consequences of Sin" in his classic book *Basic Christianity, Second Edition*-(Downers Grove: InterVarsity Press, 1971), pp. 71-80.

[9]"The Lausanne Covenant," in J.D. Douglas, Editor, Let the Earth Hear His Voice (Minneapolis: World Wide Publications, 1973), pp. 4-5.

[10]Derek Tidball, *The Social Context of the New Testament* (Grand Rapids: Zondervan, 1984), pp. 73-74.

CHAPTER 5

The Holy God Touches an Unholy House

In the year of King Uzziah's death, I saw the Lord sitting on a throne, lofty and exalted, with the train of His robe filling the temple. Seraphim stood above Him, each having six wings; with two he covered his face, and with two he covered his feet, and with two he flew. And one called out to another and said, 'Holy, Holy, Holy, is the Lord of hosts, the whole earth is full of His glory.' And the foundations of the thresholds trembled at the voice of him who called out, while the temple was filling with smoke. Then I said, 'Woe is me, for I am ruined! Because I am a man of unclean lips, and I live among a people of unclean lips; for my eyes have seen the King, the Lord of hosts.' Then one of the seraphim flew to me, with a burning coal in his hand which he had taken from the altar with tongs. And he touched my mouth with it and said, 'Behold, this has touched your lips; and your iniquity is taken away, and your sin is forgiven.' Then I heard the voice of the Lord, saying, 'Whom shall I send, and who will go for Us?' Then I said, 'Here am I. Send me!'
— Isaiah 6:1-8 —

Imagine looking through the eyes of Isaiah as he directly experienced the holiness of God. He had the great privilege of entering the very presence of God. He did not receive a message from God through an angel nor hear God's voice, but he actually had the opportunity to see God. God is so unlike his creation that Isaiah had difficulty describing him.

Holy, Holy, Holy is the Lord

Isaiah sees God sitting on a throne, and there is something very unusual about the robe the Lord was wearing. The train of His robe was filling the temple! A train worn by kings or high ranking dignitaries in their stately processions symbolized their royalty. We might imagine God's robe overlapping the throne, piling up on the floor and filling the corners of the temple. The train of his robe was everywhere revealing God's royalty.

Next Isaiah describes some very strange and peculiar beings. They were six-winged creatures called seraphim (burning ones). They in some ways were similar to Isaiah in that they had hands, feet, and faces. Yet they were very different with their six wings and their ability to fly. Four of the seraphim's six wings covered portions of their bodies.[1] The other two wings were used to fly about the throne as they sang, "Holy, Holy, Holy, is the Lord of hosts. The whole earth is full of His glory."

An educational means often employed by the Jewish people was repetition. Words were often repeated to express emphasis. Occasionally when Jesus spoke he would say, "Truly, truly" (or "Verily, verily"). This form of communication was used to stress the worth or importance of what was about to be said. Jesus was indicating that what he was about to say was very important. There are only two accounts in the entire Bible where "holy" is repeated three times. One account is in Revelation 4:8 and the other is here in Isaiah 6:3. "Holy, holy, holy," the threefold utterance regarding God's holiness, was used to indicate what is most important about the nature of God.

Woe Is Me

The foundations of the temple shook and the temple filled with smoke. The whole experience was very frightening. Isaiah was in the presence of God and began to sense God's awesome holiness through the manifestation of his glory and royalty. Strange creatures were flying around singing of God's holiness and the building was shaking and filling with smoke! If I was in a building like that one, I would suspect an earthquake accompanied by fire, as if from a volcanic crater. I would also be terrified and looking for an exit. Isaiah was not looking for the way out, but he was full of terror.

Up to this point in the passage, the one sitting on the throne had not spoken. But by being in God's holy presence, Isaiah arrived at two important conclusions. One was related to himself and the other to his neighbors. First he said, "Woe is me, for I am ruined!" Another appropriate translation for "ruined" would be "I am falling apart" or "disintegrating." Isaiah was terrified about being in the presence of God. But why would Isaiah make such a statement? Isaiah tells us: "Because I am a man of unclean lips." How did he know this? How was he able to come to this conclusion? Furthermore, he made a statement with regard to the people he lived around: "And I live among a people of unclean lips." Why did Isaiah conclude and confess both his and the people's uncleanness? We could easily understand how Isaiah could make his conclusions if God pointed His holy finger at Isaiah and said, "You are an unclean vessel!" But God had not yet spoken.

The Impact of God's Holy Presence

Had the seraphim told him that he and the people were "of unclean lips?" In a way, yes, as they called back and forth to one another, "Holy, Holy, Holy, is the Lord of hosts, the whole earth is full of His glory." But being in the actual presence of God made the difference. *No one enters the very presence of God and remains uncertain of his or her sinfulness; no one enters the very presence of God and remains unchanged – no one.* God is pure and holy, one who has no sin, no blemish, no fault, no error, and has no limitation beyond the constraints of his very nature. He is and is declared to be by those who served in His presence "Holy, Holy, Holy."

What is it about the presence of God (even when he does not speak) that brought terror into Isaiah? It is God's essence – *Holiness.* Not the concept of holiness, but the experience of being in the very presence of God's pure holiness as an unholy creature. In God's presence Isaiah discovered that he was unholy, unholy, unholy. *No one enters the very presence of God and remains uncertain of his or her sinfulness; no one enters the very presence of God and remains unchanged – no one.*

Isaiah was not the only one who had difficulty dealing with the presence of God. Look for instance at Job 40:1-4. You may recall that Job wanted the opportunity to meet with God. When he did all Job could say was, "Behold, I am insignificant; what can I reply to Thee? I lay my hand on my mouth." Consider Peter's fishing experience with Jesus recorded in Luke 5:8-11. Peter had just experienced the greatest fish catch in his life and he asked the Lord to leave because Peter realized he himself was a sinful man. Upon being confronted by the risen Lord on the road to Damascus, Saul, who later became the Apostle Paul, was blinded and thrown to the ground and could not eat or drink for days while the others with him became speechless (Acts 9:4-9). Jesus' disciples became very fearful when Jesus calmed a storm at sea and non-Christians asked Jesus to leave their region after he had finished casting out demons from the people (Mark 4:40-41 and 5:15-17, respectively). All of these individuals had difficulty dealing with pure holiness.

Interestingly, holiness is not only the nature of God but we are specifically commanded to possess it as well: "Be holy for I am holy" (Leviticus 11:44-45; 19:2; 20:7; and 1 Peter 1:14-16). But how can we be holy? When we acknowledge the presence of God, we come to know our sinfulness and are given the ability to turn from it and to be cleansed from all unrighteousness. Through this ongoing process we grow in practical holiness. This too is a part of what happens when we acknowledge and live in the presence of God.

Holiness carries with it not only an absence of sin but also a sense of judgment on sin. Holiness opposes and judges sin whenever and wherever sin is encountered. The holiness of God necessitates justice. "But who can endure the day of His coming? And who can stand when He appears? For He is like a refiner's fire and like fullers' soap" (Malachi 3:2). "Who may ascend into the hill of the Lord? And who may stand in His holy place?" (Psalm 24:3). What is the answer to these questions? "He who has clean hands and a pure heart, Who has not lifted up his soul to falsehood, And has not sworn deceitfully" (Psalm 24:4). Apparently, Isaiah did not qualify. But as soon as Isaiah acknowledged his uncleanness, he was cleansed. Then, and only then, was Isaiah ready for service. The vital point here is that only as we acknowledge and live in God's presence are we prepared for service. This is not a one time event nor is it something we do in the morning called a 'quiet time'. Rather, acknowledging and living in God's presence must be experienced moment-by-moment, day in and day out, as a life-long process. The unclean lips of both non-Christians and Christians cannot praise the One seated on the throne. But we who live in the presence of God will not only be made aware of our sinful and dependent state but will also be freed to praise and serve God.

The holiness of God reminds us that we are not holy and that our sins must be judged. Consequently, we feel fear and want to flee to avoid judgment. But it is the love and kindness (Romans 2:4) of God that draws us close to Him. It seems contradictory for on the one hand God's love draws us close to him while on the other hand we shrink away from him due to his holiness and our sinfulness. The answer to this dilemma lies in the finished work of Christ on the cross. Christ paid the penalty for our sin and, therefore, we are no longer guilty (Romans 3:25). So in Christ we are no longer judged and can boldly enter the presence of God (Romans 8:1 and Hebrews 10:18-22). It is the finished work of Christ on the cross that eliminates our fear and transforms it into awe and reverence, even joy, as we acknowledge the presence of God. We can acknowledge his presence without fear and we can remain there without condemnation (Romans 8:1)!

The Great Commandment Must Be Our First Priority

There is much activity today that is supposed to be for the glory of God but is merely performed in the flesh and, therefore, does not promote His glory. We attempt fulfilling the Great Commission without living the Great Commandment. When the focus on the Great Commission becomes a task rather than a lifestyle, then we set ourselves up for burnout and unnecessary frustration. We can only be effective in ministry when our service grows out of acknowledging and living in the presence of God. The Great Commission grows out of the Great Commandment. The Great Commission is a fruit of our lives in Christ not a task we do apart from him. Ultimately, the intention of the Great Commission is to help people obey the Great Commandment.

Summary

Many of us attempt to live lives pleasing to God and to minister for him. But we attempt to make changes in our own power without appealing to God. If our lives are to be pleasing to God we must allow him to deal with our selfishness and independence – our sinfulness. However, this self appraisal and rebuilding cannot be performed in our own power or apart from God. Acknowledging God's presence is necessary. To be content with only spending twenty to thirty minutes with God in the morning and then to go through the rest of the day not even aware of His presence is not only void of Scriptural support but is also very unwise.

Notes

[1]Wherever we find people encountering the presence of God, whether it is a Moses on Mt. Sinai or a Saul on the road to Damascus, reverence, awe, and fear are the common responses. Perhaps the seraphim covering themselves with four of their wings is an expression of humility in the presence of the One seated on the throne.

CHAPTER 6

Abiding: The House's Foundation

Paul once asked a searching question: "Who will set me free from the body of this death?" (Romans 7:24). He did not ask "what" would set him free and he certainly did not indicate that he could do anything about his problem. He asked "who" would set him free. The answer? What is the only solution to Paul's, and our, dilemma?

> Thanks be to God, through Jesus Christ our Lord!... There is therefore now no condemnation for those who are in Christ Jesus. (Romans 7:25-8:1)

As we discovered in Chapter 4, the Christian has a desire to please God but is sometimes unable to act upon this desire and ends up doing the things he does not want to do. But the good news is that when the Christian is abiding in Christ he can both *desire* to please God and also *choose* to please God.

In this chapter we examine the focal point of our Christian lives: abiding in Christ. Once abiding in Christ becomes a living reality in our lives, we will then be the kinds of persons we are created to be.

Jesus declared that his purpose and ministry for mankind's liberation was prophesied and outlined by the prophet Isaiah (Luke 4:18). The gospels show this to be the case. For Jesus' earthly mission was finished on the cross (John 19:30), manifested through his resurrection, and subsequently being demonstrated through the lives of his disciples. Jesus modeled his approach to whole-person discipleship by identifying himself with those who wanted change (Mark 2:17). We all need change but many of us do not want it or are unaware of our need.

The key for experiencing the abundant life through whole- person discipleship is that of abiding in Christ. The code of conduct for discipleship is holiness. This code of conduct can be traced back to Abraham, for Abraham was chosen to be the father of a holy nation. This was a primary reason for God's call upon his life. Holiness is also the primary call on our lives today: "You shall be holy, for I am holy" (1 Peter 1:16). Holiness means being totally set apart for God and his service. In other words, our total being is laid at the Savior's feet for him to do with as he sees fit. This holistic submission gives further thrust for discipleship that provides our total and complete liberation. Our total humanity must become fully sanctified; discipleship must not be separated from our total humanity. To share Christ is to acknowledge and to give people humanity; i.e., to help recover what Adam lost. J.D. Douglas summarizes these connections well:

> We affirm that God is both the Creator and the Judge of all men. We therefore should share his concern for justice and reconciliation throughout human society and for the liberation of men from every kind of oppression. Because mankind is made in the image of God, every person, regardless of race, religion, color, culture, class, sex or age, has an intrinsic dignity because of which he should be respected and served, not exploited . . . . The message of salvation implies a message of judgment upon every form of alienation, oppression and discrimination, and we should not be afraid to denounce evil and injustice wherever they exist. When people receive Christ they are born again into his kingdom and must seek not only to exhibit but also to spread its righteousness in the midst of an unrighteous world. The salvation we claim should be transforming us in the totality of our personal and social responsibilities. Faith without works is dead.[1]

Whole-person discipleship is more than conversion. It focuses not only on the new birth but also on the new *life* in Christ. Discipleship may be a personal response, but it is not a private experience. It is a journey of abiding in Christ where we discover the liberating elements of Christ's redemptive work in our lives regardless of our surroundings or culture.

Limitations Within Each Dimension

Due to the fall of Adam, each one of our six dimensions manifests/shares particular limitations which keep us from experiencing the abundant, fruitful life in Christ. We have at least three different types of limitations. The first is *design limitations*. This can be illustrated by walking to a cliff and jumping off; God has not given human beings the ability to fly without additional equipment. The second is *developmental limitations*. They begin at conception and continue through childhood and on into adulthood. As we grow and mature, all six dimensions of our humanity continue to develop. For example, a six-year-old child is unable to think abstractly but once he reaches the age of about 12 his mental ability has so developed that abstract thinking is possible. The third type is related to *sinfulness limitations* (total depravity). This is illustrated in our inability to live a life pleasing to God – a righteous life. The first two limitations can often be altered or directed through technology and an understanding of human development, but the third can only be dealt with by the liberating work of the Son of God. It is this third type of limitation to which whole-person discipleship directly applies.

Whole-Person Disciplemaking

Whole-person disciplemaking can be defined as the process by which a Christian, enabled by the Holy Spirit, helps another person discover the strengths and limitations of the dimensions of his life and then helps to create and encourage an atmosphere in which the individual can develop strengths and minimize various limitations as he grows in an intimate, abiding relationship with Christ. This process results in a fruitful and abundant life in Christ. It is vital that we look for strengths first, for when we acknowledge the strengths of others and help them to develop them, they are more open to what we have to say about their weaknesses and how the weaknesses detract from the contribution of the person's strengths in God's kingdom.

Bondage Positionally and Practically

Christ's liberation of man was total and complete. However, the nonbeliever still remains under bondage both positionally and practically. Believers only live under the bondage of practical limitations. Positionally, Christians are redeemed and have eternal life. Yet, part of our pilgrimage on earth is to deepen our intimacy with the Father and therefore live out a fruitful life (John 15:1-11 and Galatians 5:22-23). The total liberation is already complete and perfect (positionally), yet we become more and more liberated (practically) as we abide in Christ in all six dimensions. Thus, the dimensions of life will continue to lose the baggage acquired from the fall as we abide in Christ. We are all abiders. Some of us abide in ourselves (the flesh), someone else, or something else. But to abide in Christ is to experience Christ and to experience Christ is to live an abundant and fruitful life to the glory of God. Dietrich Bonhoeffer said:

> Discipleship means adherence to Christ, and because Christ is the object of that adherence, it must take the form of discipleship. An abstract Christology, a doctrinal system, a general religious knowledge on the subject of grace or on the forgiveness of sins, render discipleship superfluous, and in

fact they positively exclude any idea of discipleship whatever, and are essentially inimical to the whole conception of following Christ.[2]

Paul says, "Do you not know that those who run in a race all run, but only one receives the prize? Run in such a way that you may win" (1 Corinthians 9:24). Paul exhorts us to throw off the particular baggage that hinders us in running the race. The entrance to true life is revealed as we abide in Christ. To abide in Christ requires denying self. As Dietrich Bonhoeffer pointedly states:

> The disciple must say to himself the same words Peter said of Christ when he denied him: "I know not this man." Self-denial is never just a series of isolated acts of mortification or asceticism. It is not suicide, for there is an element of self-will even in that. To deny oneself is to be aware only of Christ and no more of self, to see only him who goes before and no more the road which is too hard for us. Once more, all that self-denial can say is: "He leads the way, keep close to him."[3]

Since Christ has already done the work of liberation, our lifestyle must be directed to helping people discover this liberation and how to live within it. This is true discipleship, a fulfillment of the Great Commission.

Determining the Foundation

> Therefore everyone who hears these words of Mine, and acts upon them, may be compared to a wise man, who built his house upon the rock. And the rain descended, and the floods came, and the winds blew, and burst against that house; and yet it did not fall, for it had been founded upon the rock. And everyone who hears these words of Mine, and does not act upon them, will be like a foolish man, who built his house upon the sand. And the rain descended, and the floods came, and the winds blew, and burst against that house; and it fell, and great was its fall. (Matthew 7:24-27)

I had the opportunity to work for a Christian contractor while living and ministering in Ohio among collegians. I prayed that before I left this part-time position I would have the opportunity to be involved in building a house from beginning to end. I remember the morning we went out to the field and staked out markers for the digging of the foundation. But before the foundation could be built it was necessary that we all knew what kind of house the owner wanted us to build.

If you have ever built a new house you may remember describing to the builder what kind of house you wanted. The house we built was a ranch-style house, and the owner knew where he wanted the kitchen, bathrooms, living room, and bedrooms. The style of the house determines the type of foundation necessary for it to be built upon. Once that is determined, the foundation may be dug. The kind of house determines what type of foundation is to be dug.

This construction sequence holds true when we think about the house illustration described in Chapter 1. If we want a God-like house, we need Christ as our foundation. Matthew 7:24-27 describes the building of two houses. The two houses were probably in many ways very similar. Each had a door, some windows, and a roof. But there was one main distinction between them: one house was built on sand and the other was built upon rock. Note that storms came upon both houses. What enabled one house to stand up against the rains, floods, and winds that came crashing against it yet destroyed the second house? What made the difference? According to the passage the only difference was the foundation. One house was built on a sound and solid foundation which enabled it to endure the storms and stresses of life. The other was not built to withstand storms: sand makes a very poor foundation for anything to stand upon much less stand against any storms that come upon it. The builder received a different type of blueprint from the wise man than he received from the foolish man. The foolish man was content with a foundation of sand while the wise man required a house built upon rock.

Peter describes Jesus as "A CHOICE STONE, A PRECIOUS CORNERSTONE" (1 Peter 2:6-8). The cornerstone is the first stone laid when building a foundation. The cornerstone sets and determines the direction for the entire foundation and assures that the foundation is true and straight. Jesus – and Jesus alone – is the only foundation worth building our lives upon. Everything and everyone else we attempt to build upon will eventually turn to sand and result in our destruction.

Our Life's Foundation Determines the Fruit

The parallel between building a physical house that will endure the storms of the environment and that of building a spiritual house which is honoring to God is great. Each of our "houses" exhibit particular kinds of responses when the storms of life come. Lives built upon sand will exhibit the fruit of the flesh such as that cataloged in Galatians 5:19-21: immorality, impurity, sensuality, idolatry, sorcery, enmities, strife, jeal-

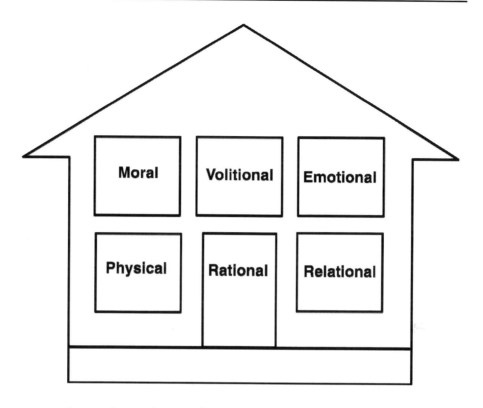

ousy, outbursts of anger, disputes, dissensions, factions, envying, drunkenness, carousing ("partying"), and other character traits like them. But the lives built upon Jesus Christ, the Rock and Cornerstone of our faith, will exhibit entirely different kinds of fruit, indeed the fruit of the Spirit: love, joy, peace, patience, kindness, goodness, faithfulness, gentleness, self-control (Galatians 5:21-22). The foundation chosen not only provides the necessary structural support that enables the house to stand, but it also determines what type of fruit will be seen through the windows.

If we want our lives to exhibit the fruit of the Spirit, we must abide in Christ. There is no other way to manifest the fruit of the Spirit in our lives. Jesus made this very clear:

> I am the true vine, and My Father is the vinedresser. Every branch in Me that does not bear fruit, He takes away; and every branch that bears fruit, he prunes it, that it may bear more fruit. You are already clean because of the word which I have spoken to you. Abide in Me, and I in you. As the branch cannot bear fruit of itself, unless it abides in the vine, so neither can

you, unless you abide in Me. I am the vine, you are the branches; he who abides in Me, and I in him, he bears much fruit; for apart from me you can do nothing. If anyone does not abide in Me, he is thrown away as a branch, and dries up; and they gather them, and cast them into the fire, and they are burned. If you abide in Me, and My words abide in you, ask whatever you wish, and it shall be done for you. By this is My Father glorified, that you bear much fruit, and so prove to be My disciples. Just as the Father has loved Me, I have also loved you; abide in My love. If you keep My commandments, you will abide in My love; just as I have kept My Father's commandments, and abide in His love. These things I have spoken to you, that My joy may be in you, and that your joy may be made full. (John 15:1-11)

Every Christian abides in Christ in a positional sense. As members of God's family, we reside in his family. Our standing and position before God cannot be altered – we will always be a member of God's family through the blood of Christ. We might call this "positional abiding." But a second type of abiding, the practice of abiding or "practical abiding," is a choice on our part. Practical abiding is acknowledging and living in Christ's presence moment-by-moment. We are always choosing which type of foundation we are living on – sand, which is soft and always shifting about, or rock, which is solid and firm. Having once chosen to set our lives on the Rock, we can at anytime (and frequently do!) move away from living upon the Rock and step into the vagaries of life on the sand. Jesus stresses the practice of abiding by making it a command: "Abide in Me" (John 15:4). Practical abiding does not occur automatically, we chose this form of abiding: "If you abide in Me . . ." (John 15:7).

For example, each of my four children were born into our family and will, therefore, always be a member of our family: this is their standing or position in the family. Yet as they get older, they spend less and less time with my wife, Darlene, and me. The intimacy we once had is not as frequent. They are still members of the Sabo family, but practically speaking a void is present. Their positional status cannot be altered, but their practical moment-by-moment interactions are influenced by the choices they make.

A Fleshly Foundation Can Only Produce Fruit of the Flesh

Take special note of Jesus' words at the end of the passage in John 15:1-11: "These things I have spoken to you, that My joy may be in you, and that your joy may be made full." Joy is tied to abiding in Christ. There is a direct relationship between abiding in Christ and experiencing full joy. Just as the foundation of a house enables it to withstand storms, so abiding in Christ enables the Christian to respond to the daily pressures, trials, tribulations, and decisions of life. When the fruit of the flesh is seen through the windows of our lives, we can be certain that we are at that moment abiding in our flesh and not in Christ.

In Hosea 10:1 the nation of Israel is portrayed as a luxuriant vine that produces fruit for itself. God was not pleased with Israel's state nor is he pleased with the non-Christian's state. Until an individual becomes a Christian, he is the vine and produces fruit for himself – fleshly fruit. But once an individual becomes a Christian, the days of being the vine are over. The individual becomes a branch abiding in the vine – Christ. We have been created to produce fruit not for self but that which is honoring to God. But when a Christian abides in self (the flesh), the fruit that results is the opposite of the fruit of the Spirit (Galatians 5:17-21).

Too often we are asking, telling, and even demanding that we and others produce the fruit of the Spirit through the power of the flesh – human effort. Such a request is impossible to fulfill. Why? The fruit of the flesh comes natural to the flesh; the flesh naturally produces fleshly fruit. No one can exhibit godly, supernatural fruit by the power of the flesh. Each tree is known by its own fruit. Each plant produces fruit in accordance with its own design and nature:

> For there is no good tree which produces bad fruit; nor, on the other hand, a bad tree which produces good fruit. For each tree is known by its own fruit. For men do not gather figs from thorns, nor do they pick grapes from a briar bush. The good man out of the good treasure of his heart brings forth what is good; and the evil man out of the evil treasure brings forth what is evil; for his mouth speaks from that which fills his heart. (Luke 6:43-45)

This passage in Luke helps us to understand what Paul teaches in Romans 3:10-17, especially verse 12. Goodness has its source in God; God is the only one who is good (Luke 18:18-19). Since no one is good, the only way one can do good is to somehow connect (abide) with God enabling goodness to flow from God to and through a person.

Focus on Christ Not His Fruit

We confuse and mislead both ourselves and others when we sum up the Christian life as the performing of particular activities like Bible study, Scripture memory, quiet time, prayer, worship, and witnessing. We can participate in every one of these activities apart from abiding in Christ, but the results are not honoring to God. Indeed, we cannot do anything to the glory of God apart from abiding in Him (John 15:5). Attempting to produce supernatural fruit by our own efforts (in the flesh) leads to a life of frustration and will cause us to wonder why we are not living a God-like life.

So, we must avoid a second common error. Not only is shallowness and emptiness the result of a life focused on external "religious" activity, but the same is true when our focus is on the fruit of the Spirit as the end. We forget that the fruit of the Spirit comes naturally (or *supernaturally*) as we abide. Our focus is on Christ not on the results of being in his presence. Similarly, individuals spend time in the sun to get a suntan. The suntan results by being in the rays of the sun for an extended period of time. It is the fruit of being in the presence of the sun. What we must remember is that the fruit of the Spirit is like the suntan, but our focus is not the suntan but the Son. We must avoid trying to use the Son to get what is simply an expression, a result, of being in his presence. We are to be captivated with *him* not what he gives us.

When Moses (Exodus 34:29-35) came down off Mount Sinai, his face glowed. Why? Because he was in the presence of pure light, he assumed some of the characteristics of the one he was with - the Lord. Since we cannot make supernatural fruit appear in our lives, we must stop trying! We can, however, and are able to abide in Christ. Abide in Christ and the fruit will come.

Imagine walking into an orchard full of orange trees. What is one sure way you know there is life in an orange tree? When there are oranges on the tree. An orange tree can exist without producing oranges, but in such cases the orange tree is not functioning according to the Creator's original plan – fruit bearing. Orange trees are created to produce oranges. Similarly, we are designed to live abundant lives to the glory of God. This abundant living occurs when the fruit of the Spirit is seen in our lives. Have you ever heard orange trees groaning to produce oranges? Probably not. Rather, as the branches remain connected to the main trunk of the orange tree, the life- giving sap of the tree flows into the branches and, as long as the branch remains (abides) in the vine, the sap keeps flowing and builds up so much in the branch that it comes bursting through in the form of oranges. The branch of the orange tree which does not remain connected to the vine is like the non-Christian or the Christian who does not abide in Christ. The result is not fruit of the godly supernatural type but fruit of the flesh.

You may recall that when Isaiah was in the presence of God he encountered his sin and depravity at a frightening depth (Isaiah 6). John records Isaiah saying that he saw Jesus' glory (John 12:41). It was the holy presence of God that brought Isaiah to the terrifying conclusion regarding his own unworthiness and shame. Isaiah became humbly aware of who he really was in contrast to God. *No one acknowledges the presence of the glorified Christ and remains unchanged – no one!* The non-Christian often becomes hardened and attempts to run from or deny the presence of God while Christian's have the privilege of enjoying God's presence and serving him gladly. As we acknowledge and abide in his presence, we become humble and fruitful.

The Phantom Police Car

Imagine that I am a passenger in a friend's car as he drives to work. As we talk, I notice through the side mirror that a police car is following us. I say nothing but continue our conversation. A couple of minutes later my friend gets a horrified look on his face as he glances in his rear-view mirror. As he slams on his brakes he yells, "Oh no! A cop!" I respond, "What's wrong? The police officer has been following you for the last five minutes." My friend replies, "But I didn't know it; if I had known he was behind me, I would have slowed down a long time ago!" Even though the police officer had been following my friend for quite some time, his presence had no real effect until my friend acknowledged it. Once my friend perceived the officer's presence, he chose to act and live (drive) accordingly.

When I was a young boy there was a television commercial called "Remember the Phantom Police Car." The main idea of the commercial was to encourage drivers to imagine a police car, even though they could not see it, was right alongside of them. If drivers acted as though there was a police cruiser alongside of them, the idea was that they would be more likely to obey the speed limits and other laws.

Here are two incidents from my own life, one of defeat and one of victory, which explore this idea. I needed to talk to one of my children regarding an issue that was potentially very volatile. I remember praying as I walked to my teenager's bedroom asking the Lord to help me be self-controlled (a fruit of the Spirit). I was not in the bedroom for more than two or three minutes before both I and my teenager exhibited an abundance of fleshly fruit. I remember walking back to my bedroom thinking that prayer does not work! I had asked God to help me be self-controlled, but look what happened. I did the very thing I didn't want to do! The whole event was a mystery to me because I knew I had the potential to lose my temper; that's why I had asked God to help me. As I walked into the room I remember saying to myself, "Relax, be in control, you must be self-controlled," but I completely lost it. I was really perplexed. What had happened? Why didn't God help me? Not long after my failure I realized that I was attempting to manifest the fruit of the Spirit by myself. Once this truth gripped me, I had the solution to my baffling questions. To me, God was not in the room, just my teenager and I. That was the problem. He was there, but I did not acknowledge his presence and abide in him.

I had a second conversation with the same child. It was also a conversation that had the potential to explode – at the atomic level. This time I did not throw a prayer to God as I walked to the room. Instead, I spoke with my heavenly Father as he walked into the room with me. I did not think about being self-controlled, but I focused on "taking every thought captive to the obedience of Christ" (2 Corinthians 10:5). Instead of having a dialogue with my teenager, I was in the midst of a *trialogue* between my teenager and my heavenly Father. Three of us were present in that room. My teenager still acted in a volatile manner, but as I left the room I marveled at the self-control and kindness that I had exhibited – what the Spirit had exhibited through me as I abided in Christ. Like Isaiah, I was aware of my own state of depravity and at the same time the depth of Jesus' holiness. By practicing the presence of Christ rather than focusing upon spiritual fruit, the fruit of the Spirit was supernaturally demonstrated through my life. Too many of us, however, more easily relate to Jacob who woke up after a dream and announced, "Surely the Lord is in this place, and I did not know it" (Genesis 28:10-17). We need to acknowledge his presence even more than we need to acknowledge the presence of a phantom police officer. Surely God is with us, but do we know it?

Lights that Shine

The One that people see when we abide in Christ is the Holy Spirit. You might say, "Wait a minute, the Holy Spirit is invisible so you can't see Him." You are correct, but he does dwell within every believer and he does exhibit identifiable characteristics. These characteristics are his fruit, the identifiable marks of the Holy Spirit. The need on our part is to get self out of the way in order that the Spirit may be seen. When we deny our self (Luke 9:23), the fruit of the flesh is no longer seen and the Spirit's characteristics come shining through the windows of our lives. Denying self comes very quickly in the presence of God. *No one remains bold, arrogant, and rebellious when he encounters the holiness of God – no one.*

As we abide in Christ, the abundant life he brings to our lives flows supernaturally into our minds where we formulate beliefs, attitudes, and values. Our minds (door)

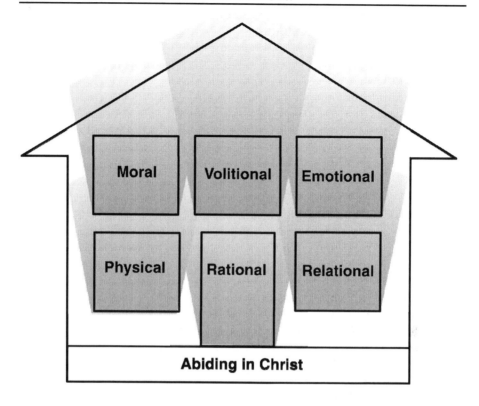

are in the process of being renewed (Romans 12:1-2) by the Holy Spirit. This renewing process is seen in the tangible expression of the Spirit's fruit throughout the windows of our lives.

As we abide, we begin to have beliefs, attitudes, and values that are godly. These then come shining through our lives for the world to see. Our renewed minds lead to renewed living. What people see is not our fruit, but supernatural fruit flowing from those captivated with Christ. This is Christ working in and through us.

The impact of the abiding process touches all of who and what we are. As we abide in Christ, our responses to the everyday trials and worries of life flow from Christ through the door and windows of our lives brightly shining for the world to see.

God Moving Towards Man

One of my wife's favorite songs is "When a Man Loves a Woman."[4] In the song, a man tells how he goes through all types of difficulties to express his love for the woman of his dreams. He says he cannot keep his mind on anything other than his love and that he would give up all his comforts for the sake of the woman. These lyrics remind me of Jesus' great love for us:

> [Christ Jesus], although he existed in the form of God, did not regard equality with God a thing to be grasped, but emptied Himself, taking the form of a bond-servant, and being made in the likeness of men. And being found in appearance as a man, He humbled Himself by becoming obedient to the point of death, even death on a cross. (Philippians 2:6-8)

Truly God loves us! You could say the Bible is God's love song recording the great lengths he has gone to in order to show his love for humanity all the way to the ultimate expression of his love in the giving of his only son's life for our salvation.

As I trace the sequence of God moving closer and closer to humanity, I see the real intent of his love and motivation. In the Old Testament we read about how our Creator God walked and talked intimately with Adam and Eve. It was a very close relationship between the Creator and Adam and Eve. But sin entered humanity and the once cherished intimacy with God was severed. In spite of this severing due to sin, God made a promise of future intimacy in Christ. Later God called out from his lofty heavenly residence to a mere creature residing in Ur named Abram. God was no longer walking alongside of humanity but called out to him from heaven. This is the beginning of God moving towards humanity by talking with Abram and making promises to him. God moved closer when he met Moses on Mount Sinai. God came down from the heavenlies and met Moses on earth, but the presence of God did not go with Moses for when Moses left the mount, the only thing that he took with him was the shining of his face. Even though the Lord himself led the children of Israel out from Egypt in a pillar of cloud by day and in a pillar of fire at night (Exodus 13:21; 14:19,24; 33:7-11), it was not the same kind of face-to-face intimacy Moses had experienced on the mountain. The Lord moved even closer to humanity as is seen in his willingness to reside in the holy of holies of the traveling tabernacle, however, only the High Priest could meet with him and then only once a year. Later Solomon built a more permanent residence for God, the Temple. Even so humanity was still separated from the presence of God by a veil, in both Tabernacle and Temple. It served as a reminder of the distance between God's holiness and humanity's sinfulness and unworthiness to enter the Lord's immediate presence. In the New Testament era, God took on the form of humanity in the person of Jesus of Nazareth and he lived and walked among humankind. The final expression of humanity's union and intimacy with God was yet to come. Through the death of Christ, God in the person of the Holy Spirit enters and dwells within human temples – individual Christians.

Thank you, Lord, that even though we are unworthy, through the blood of the Lamb of God, you made intimacy – an abiding relationship with you – once again a possibility for humanity, even me.

Knowing Christ Experientially

Paul made some amazing, truly profound statements. Consider the following passage:

> But whatever things were gain to me, those things I have counted as loss for the sake of Christ. More than that, I count all things to be loss in view of the surpassing value of knowing Christ Jesus my Lord, for whom I have suffered the loss of all things, and count them but rubbish in order that I may gain Christ, and may be found in Him, not having a righteousness of my own derived from the Law, but that which is through faith in Christ, the righteousness which comes from God on the basis of faith, that I may know Him and the power of His resurrection and the fellowship of His sufferings, being conformed to His death; in order that I may attain to the resurrection from the dead. (Philippians 3:7-12)

Just prior to these statements, Paul listed his very impressive credentials: "… circumcised the eighth day, of the nation of Israel, of the tribe of Benjamin, a Hebrew of Hebrews; as to the Law, a Pharisee; as to zeal, a persecutor of the church; as to the righteousness which is in the Law, found blameless" (Philippians 3:5-6). Even though he had all these things, Paul judges that they amounted to nothing in comparison to knowing Christ. Paul was eager to lose what the world says is a satisfying life to gain what God says is the abundant life – intimacy with His Son.

But what does Paul mean by knowing Christ? The focal point of Paul's message is not an intellectual understanding of Christ, but one of personal experience, of personal relationship. There is a significant difference between knowing about someone and knowing them intimately. Knowledge about someone can be accomplished by merely gathering facts, but to have personal experience of someone means more than the accumulation of facts. This should come as no surprise to us, particularly in light of the Great Commandment:

Teacher, which is the great commandment in the Law? And He said to him, 'YOU SHALL LOVE THE LORD YOUR GOD WITH ALL YOUR HEART, AND WITH ALL YOUR SOUL, AND WITH ALL YOUR MIND.' This is the great and foremost commandment. (Matthew 22:36-38)

Jesus was quoting Deuteronomy 6:5 where it records Moses' teaching the Israelites the Law of God just before they entered the promised land. The idea in both the Old and New Testaments is one of priority and holism. God must be first, but he also wants all of who and what we are. To be human requires that we have a physical body, moral standards, the ability to choose, emotions, relational capacities as well as a mind. All of these are to be submitted to God and brought into a relationship with him. We can no longer be content to know Bible verses about him or to know the stories of the Bible or even to tell others about him; rather, we must walk intimately with Him.

Paul believed and taught that to really live life is to know Christ experientially. What does it mean to experience Christ? I just suggested that our Lord requires all of who and what we are. Thinking of the house illustration, we can say that the whole house, not just the door, is used to experience him. To experience him we employ the use of our five senses: hearing, sight, smell, taste, and touch. Our senses enable us to encounter God's creation. They also enable us to encounter the Creator. After all, the Lord gave us all of our capacities to use and to glorify Him. Paul tells us that "whether, then, you eat or drink or whatever you do, do all to the glory of God" (1 Corinthians 10:31). In other words, there is nothing that we are or possess that cannot be and should not be used to God's glory.

The winner of four academy awards including best picture, *Chariots of Fire* [5] portrays the exciting true story of Harold Abrahams' and Eric Liddell's quest for an Olympic gold medal. Eric Liddell and his sister, Jenny, were both making plans to go to China to spread the word of God, but there was a source of tension between Eric and Jenny. Eric was a very fine runner and was training for the Olympics. His sister was very dedicated to ministering for God and was preparing to move to China. At one point in the movie Jenny shares her concern that Eric may have lost his vision for the ministry. Eric assures Jenny that he had not, but that he also could not deny that God had made him fast and that when he ran he felt God's pleasure. If you are a jogger or runner, do you sense God's pleasure when you run? When you are working on your car or washing the dishes, do you sense the presence of God?

I have played racquetball for nineteen years and at one time was a local club pro. I have had the privilege of playing four different professional racquetball players and three of them were national champions. Racquetball is an explosive competitive game. The ball hit by the top ranked pros can accelerate up to 180 m.p.h. That's a fast moving game! There is very little time to think during play. In order to excel in this game, a player's reaction time must be split second and hand/eye coordination exceptional. How can I play racquetball to the glory of God? I know that the text "Do all to the glory of God" does not mean winning the game. I believe it refers to acknowledging his presence on the court and playing in such a way that honors him – both in skill and in spirit. The focus is not on self or winning but on him. If I want to exhibit the fruit of the Spirit on the court, I must be abiding in Christ while on the court. God can and should be glorified while I am playing racquetball. As I abide in Christ, I will be controlled by the Spirit of God. What is seen is not my fruit but God's fruit.

Maybe you do not play racquetball or run. Maybe you are not an athlete and sweating does not particularly excite you. Whatever you do, do it to the glory of God. As the storms of life touch us on the court, in our wallets, at the office, or in our homes, the only way the Spirit's fruit will be manifested is by abiding in Him.

The Terror & Peace of Abiding

When Isaiah entered the presence of God he became terrified. He saw his own depravity at a very deep level and became frightened. Do you remember what Peter said to Jesus after the big fish catch that was causing the boats to sink?: "he fell down at Jesus' feet, saying, 'Depart from me, for I am a sinful man, O Lord!'" (Luke 5:8). Who told Peter that he was a sinful man? Why did he want Jesus to leave? What about Saul's encounter with Jesus on the road to Damascus (Acts 9)? After falling to the ground, Saul (later Paul) asked a very interesting question: "Who art Thou, Lord?" Saul did not know the source of the blinding light or the voice that cried out to him, but he did realize that, whoever the source was, he was Lord. Note Job's response after the holy God questioned him: "Behold, I am insignificant; what can I reply to Thee? I lay my hand on my mouth" (Job 40:3). Even Adam and Eve were afraid of the presence of God in the midst of their sin (Genesis 3:8), afraid enough to try to hide from his presence. No matter who it was, whether Adam and Eve, Isaiah, Job, Peter or Saul, who came into the presence of God, they were frightened. These people were made aware of the holiness of God as well as their unworthiness to be in his presence.

Sadly, a great number of Christians today have lost any real fear (awe) of God. He is often viewed as the big daddy in the sky that will give us whatever our little hearts desire. We need the experiential truth that God is holy and without sin and that we are sinners who, apart from the shed blood of Christ on our behalf, are condemned. The psalmist puts it this way: "If you, O Lord, kept a record of sins, O Lord, who could stand? But with you there is forgiveness; therefore you are feared" (Psalm 130:3-4, NIV). This verse reminds me that I am a sinner, that God has forgiven me, and that I should fear Him. God is so unlike me or anyone I know, yet he loves me. I stand in awe of him, and when I sin instead of fearing his judgment, I can run to him due to his love, mercy, and forgiveness in Christ.

We must remember that God's holiness does not frighten a holy person, but rather the sinful person. We are sinful, unworthy, and we fear a deep intimate encounter with Christ. At the same time we are strangely drawn to his presence. Our personal sin is what causes us to run, but Jesus' love is what draws us towards him. We become frightened by so many things, and God is the One who tells us to fear not for he is with us (Isaiah 41:10). The reason we fear as Christians is because we do not acknowledge or live in his presence, but as soon as we experience his presence through abiding in Christ, we exhibit the fruit of peace (Galatians 5:22-23).

Isaiah 41:10 shows us that if we are fearful we are to call upon God. If we lack peace, we need to call upon God who is our peace (Isaiah 26:3). Peace is related to the presence of God, even to his name.

YHWH Is All Things to Those Who Follow Him

Years ago my parents took me to see Cecil B. De Mille's movie *The Ten Commandments*. I can still remember the scene vividly where Moses is standing by the burning bush and is told by God to go to Pharaoh and tell him to "let My people go." After receiving this commission from God, Moses asks God, "Now they may say to me, 'What is His name?' What shall I say to them?" And God said to Moses, 'I AM WHO I AM'; and He said, 'Thus you shall say to the sons of Israel, 'I AM has sent me to you.'" (Exodus 3:13-14). "I AM" or YHWH is God's personal name. Many of the descriptions for God in Scripture are titles or designations that depict his character or nature. For example, "Adonai" means Lord and Master (Exodus 4:10-12), "Elohim" means Mighty One (Genesis 1:1), and "El Shaddai" means All-Sufficient God (Genesis 17:1-20). But YHWH is God's personal name informing us of something about Him unlike these other titles.

English was not my favorite subject in high school. I knew, however, that there was something about God's response to Moses that did not sound quite grammatically correct. "I AM THAT I AM?" You am what? You are what? What is it that you are?

God's response sounds like a verb without an object, but grammatically the verb "to be" does not require an object. There is a very important point here that must not be overlooked: God is to us whatever we need. In a very real sense he fills in what we really need. He is . . . – you name it. Whatever is our legitimate need is exactly what God is and wants to be to us. The catch here is that it is *God* – not we – who defines what we really need him to be and when he needs to be that to us.

The following are nine examples of how God's personal name related to the needs of his people, Israel. In each case God provided something that an individual or the people lacked.

One 'technical' note on the translation of the name of God. In both the NIV and NASB, the Hebrew letters for God's personal name "YHWH" are transcribed in capital letters as "LORD". When we come across LORD we should take note what our personal heavenly Father is providing for or offering to us, his children.

YHWH Our Intimate God	
1. YHWH Jireh	YHWH will provide (Genesis 22:13-14)
2. YHWH Nissi	YHWH is my banner (Exodus 17:15)
3. YHWH Shalom	YHWH is peace (Judges 6:24)
4. YHWH Sabaoth	YHWH of hosts/armies (1 Samuel 1:3)
5. YHWH Mekaddidhkem	YHWH makes you holy (Exodus 31:13)
6. YHWH Raah	YHWH is my shepherd (Psalm 23:1)
7. YHWH Tsidkenu	YHWH is our righteousness (Jeremiah 23:6)
8. YHWH Shammah	YHWH is there (Ezekiel 48:35)
9. YHWH Rapha	YHWH your healer (Exodus 15:26)

As we grow in our realization of the Lord's gracious provision for all our needs, we will desire to abide with him throughout the day. One day that fifteen minute morning devotion just will not be enough – you will want, desire, even crave more time with him.

Union with Christ

There are numerous terms and phrases that are synonymous with abiding in Christ. One such phrase is "union with Christ."[6] The following is a reflective set of excerpts describing how one political philosopher understood the idea of union in Christ:

"The history of nations teaches us the necessity of union with Christ. . . . The examination of the individual proves the necessity of union with Christ." But as 'the last proof' he cites 'the word of Christ himself.' "Our heart, reason, history, the Word of Christ, all cry out to us loudly and convincingly that union with Him is absolutely necessary; that without Him we are unable to fulfill our purpose; that without Him we would be rejected by God; that He alone is capable of redeeming us.

As soon as we have grasped the necessity of union, the reason for it is clear to behold – our need for salvation, our sinful nature, our faltering reason, our corrupt heart, our unworthiness before God. . . . Then, when a more beautiful sun has arisen through our union with Christ, when we feel all our wickedness, but at the same time can rejoice over our salvation, only then can we love the God who formerly appeared to us as an offended ruler, but now as a forgiving Father, a kind teacher.

"Inasmuch as we have Him before our eyes and in our heart...we turn our hearts at the same time towards the brethren whom he has joined more intimately with us, and for whom, also, He has sacrificed Himself.

"This love of Christ is not fruitless. It not only fills us with the purest worship and reverence for Him, but also makes us keep His commandments . . . by being virtuous – but virtuous for love of Him...This is the great abyss which divides Christian virtue from any other, and lifts it above all others; this is one of the greatest effects which the union with Christ produces in man. ...Once a man has acquired this virtue, this union with Christ, he will await with composure the buffetings of fate, will counter bravely the storms of passion, and bear fearlessly the rage of the wicked. For who...can rob him of his Saviour? ...

"Who would not gladly suffer since he knows that through his adherence to Christ, through his deeds, God himself is being glorified...

"The union with Christ provides moral edification, consolation in sorrow, quiet confidence, and a heart open to the love of mankind, all things noble, all greatness – not for ambition, or desire for fame, but only for love of Christ."[7]

The author of this impressive essay is none other than Karl Marx. I am saddened by individuals, such as Marx, who can so beautifully articulate a deep theological truth and yet have a life that is void of it in any practical way. We all know that there is a significant difference between knowing something intellectually and experiencing or living it in practice.

Summary

The primary thrust of this chapter has been to present an understanding of what abiding in Christ means and to underscore that we need more than just an academic or intellectual understanding of it.

We live in a society that places a greater emphasis on output than input. The Church is no exception. Christians who emphasize doing instead of being usually burn out or become complacent in their faith after years of laboring under such a task-oriented Christianity. They have exchanged loving God for "making disciples" or some other activity. Refueling and refocusing are necessary. Someone once said, "Unless your input exceeds your output, your upkeep will be your downfall."

For further study in the area of abiding see Appendix G.

Notes

[1] J. D. Douglas, Editor, *Let the Earth Hear His Voice* (World Wide Publications, 1975), pp. 3-9.

[2] Dietrich Bonhoeffer, *The Cost of Discipleship* (London: SCM Press Ltd., 1959; reprinted New York: Touchstone Books, Simon & Schuster Inc., 1995), p. 63.

[3] Ibid., p. 97.

[4] Percy Sledge, *The Best of Percy Sledge* (New York: Atlantic Recording Corporation).

[5] Warner Brothers, *Chariots of Fire* (Burbank: Warner Communications Co, 1981).

[6] Two excellent books on this subject are Lewis B. Smedes, *Union with Christ* (Grand Rapids: William B. Eerdmans, 1970) and John Stott, *Life in Christ* (Grand Rapids: Baker Book House, 1996. Smedes' book is out-of-print but Stott's is still available and might also be found in used editions published by Tyndale House (Wheaton, 1991) or under the titles *Understanding Christ*-(Zondervan, 1981) or *Focus on Christ*-(Collier/Macmillan, 1979).

[7] Karl Marx, "Marx on 'Union with Christ,'" Christianity Today (June 19, 1961), p. 13.

CHAPTER 7

Laying the Foundation of Abiding

We attend a medium-sized church in the Midwest that utilizes drama as a part of its regular Sunday services. Recently we saw a multi-media slide presentation that touched me deeply.[1] It used only two clay figures to tell a story. One figure represented God and the other a man. God was sitting down. The man came walking by, encountered this being sitting down, and concluded this being is God! The man became so excited that he wanted to *give* God something. He began by bringing his house to God and anticipated God's pleased reception. But God was not pleased and the man turned away sadly. He then brought his hobbies, represented by his golf clubs, racquets, and other related sports equipment. But God turned away and communicated his displeasure. The man was disappointed but had yet another idea. He brought all his money to God, for surely God would want his money. But the response was the same and God was not pleased with the man's wealth. The man was obviously perplexed and wondered what would God want, what would please him? Oh! Yes! Now he knew and he reached into his pocket and pulled out his lucky rabbit's foot! Again God communicated His disapproval and turned away. The man was truly saddened and turned away not knowing what to give God. Then he got the idea that God did not want any of his possessions but rather wanted him to do things for Him. So the man started carrying signs that said, "God loves you" and "Judgment Day is coming!" But just as God did not seek the man's earthly possessions so He did not seek the man's activity. The man was beside himself and astonished by God's unwillingness to accept all of what he offered. What could God possibly want? What was left? Suddenly a small door opened on the man's chest and his heart began to come out. God's face shone with acceptance and, as the man gave his heart to God and embraced his heavenly Father with the most satisfied and secure expression on his face, he discovered that God did not want his possessions, abilities, or his activities: he wanted all of who and what the man was.

Too often the non-Christian attempts to buy God or satisfy him by giving him his possessions, but God is not pleased or satisfied. The Christian understands God's response because mere temporal objects will not stand the test of time or endure forever. Similarly, many Christians strive to please God by serving him. This idea sounds theologically sound and some try to support it with Scripture. Often these men and women are calling others to experience a joy and satisfaction that they themselves are not experiencing, yet they are fearful to admit or talk to others about their dissatisfaction. Furthermore, when questioned about why they spend themselves for God, they quote the Great Commission (Matthew 28:18-20) and say, "This is what I am giving my life to."

Only One Thing Is Necessary

To the Christian who attempts to please God by giving his life to the Great Commission, God's response is the same as his response to the non-Christian who seeks to win God's approval by giving him his possessions. But we have already seen that our focal point must not be the Great Commission but the Great Commandment:

> Teacher, which is the great commandment in the Law? And He said to him, YOU SHALL LOVE THE LORD YOUR GOD WITH ALL YOUR HEART, AND WITH ALL YOUR SOUL, AND WITH ALL YOUR MIND. This is the great and foremost commandment. (Matthew 22:36-38)

The solution is not found in offering God our wealth or our activity, but in giving God all of our self. This is also seen in another passage:

> Now as they were traveling along, He entered a certain village; and a woman named Martha welcomed Him into her home. And she had a sister called Mary, who moreover was listening to the Lord's word, seated at His feet. But Martha was distracted with all her preparations; and she came up to Him, and said, "Lord, do You not care that my sister has left me to do all the serving alone? Then tell her to help me." But the Lord answered and said to her, "Martha, Martha, you are worried and bothered about so many things; but only a few things are necessary, really only one, for Mary has chosen the good part, which shall not be taken away from her." (Luke 10:38-42, emphasis mine)

This passage portrays Martha as missing the most important thing in life! She was caught up so much with serving the Lord (or maybe herself) that she was missing what her sister Mary was experiencing with him. What was that experience? What was Mary enjoying that Martha was missing? *The presence of God.*

We Christians have great difficulty living in a manner that knowing Christ experientially, practicing the presence of God, is really the ultimate goal of our lives. Rather, we strive to please God by doing spiritual activities at the expense of experiencing him throughout our entire being (or to put it another way, of having God live throughout our whole house). There are too many of us involved with ministry activities who are not abiding in Christ. Think about this calming and arresting command: "Cease striving and know that I am God" (Psalm 46:10). For some reason we just do not get it. We keep on striving, just like Martha, to please God and to serve him when what the Lord really wants is just one thing! Imagine, just one thing! We live such busy, hectic lives, and there are so many things we think we must do. But Jesus said there is really only one! "What is it Jesus, please tell me and I will do it!" The answer is the same one he told Martha. The answer is the same one the Apostle Paul expounds in Philippians 3. It is the same answer articulated in Psalm 46:10. And just so we will not miss it, it is carefully explained by Jesus and recorded for us in John 15. The Psalmist exhorted us to "know" God. Mary chose to enjoy the presence of Jesus. Paul called it knowing Christ. Jesus chose to describe it as abiding. All four of these passages (and there are many more) emphasize the process of acknowledging and living in the presence of the Lord not only throughout the day but also throughout our whole being.[2]

As mentioned earlier, the movie *Chariots of Fire* portrays the exciting true story of Harold Abrahams and Eric Liddell's quest for a gold medal.[3] In the movie, right before he runs in the finals for the gold medal, Harold Abrahams admits that he has been running for himself and that he has not experienced peace or contentment. Eric Liddell's focus and desire for running was quite different from Abrahams'. This difference is seen in Liddell's unwillingness to run on Sunday, for he believed that this act would be displeasing to God by profaning the Lord's Day. You see, Liddell ran as an expression of his Christianity. More to the point, he was not driven to run for self gain but because when he ran, he experienced God's pleasure. His focus was on God more than on running. We need to move from Abrahams' running for self and move towards Liddell's running for God's pleasure. Abrahams was a man driven by many things, but Eric was one who was *drawn* by God. Liddell had discovered that there is really only one thing in life worth doing. Once we discover and live according to this truth, we will be free from the bondage of striving to experience what we ultimately already possess – fellowship and intimacy with Christ. We simply must acknowledge his presence, the awareness of His presence around us every moment of our existence, and consciously live in it.

Typically Christians who are driven are those who want to do things *for* God rather than *with* Him. Those who are driven frequently focus on events, activities, production, and results. They move from one event to another. They are consumed with the need to stuff their ministry suitcase full of spiritual activities and statistics. In so doing, they miss the process of walking with their Savior throughout life. In practice these Christians are actually involved in a form of idolatry. They have exchanged intimacy with the Father for the business of "The Ministry." The book of Ecclesiastes clearly points to the dissatisfaction of giving one's life to work; and this means any type of toil including ministry (Ecclesiastes 2:18-23 and 4:4-8).

Practical Steps to Abiding

Growing in the process of experiencing the presence of Christ has been the greatest joy of my life. But teaching others how to abide in his presence is difficult for at least three reasons. First, people are at different levels of their spiritual maturity. Second, personality and temperament are vital factors in experiencing His presence. Third, if I present a means, method, or model of abiding, it might work for some but not for others, and some will make an idol out of the method. The emphasis must not be on a method or model but rather on Christ. We do not have the responsibility to dictate, determine, or assign the methodology of abiding with Christ for another. Rather, we have the responsibility to assist others in discovering ways of abiding that are relevant to them.

In light of these three factors, I offer below brief comments on selected Bible passages pertaining to the idea of abiding in Christ, quotes from individuals referring to practicing the presence of Christ, and metaphors that attempt to clarify the meaning of abiding.

The chapter concludes with a summary of biblical principles of abiding. I believe that if a Christian understands the *principles* of abiding, and desires to abide, the Holy Spirit will lead that person in ways of abiding that are, for that person, most helpful and significant.

BIBLICAL REFERENCES & COMMENTS

The following references and comments are provided for a fuller understanding of the Biblical meaning of abiding. Each reference is followed by a comment highlighting a point related to abiding.

2 Corinthians 5:9

Therefore also we have as our ambition, whether at home or absent, to be pleasing to Him.

> **Comment:** The attitude that the abiding Christian has, is one of pleasing God. A constant attitude he has at the forefront of his mind is, "Lord I will do whatever you lead me to do?"

Psalm 25:15

My eyes are continually toward the Lord....

> **Comment:** An attitude of continual dependence is promoted here.

Exodus 33:13-16

Now therefore, I pray Thee, if I have found favor in Thy sight, let me know Thy ways, that I may know Thee, so that I may find favor in Thy sight. Consider too, that this nation is Thy people." And He said, "My presence shall go with you, and I will give you rest." Then he said to Him, "If Thy presence does not go with us, do not lead us up from here. For how then can it be known that I have found favor in Thy sight, I and Thy people? Is it not by Thy going with us, so that we, I and Thy people, may be distinguished from all the other people who are upon the face of the earth?

> **Comment:** Moses knew that the presence of God was necessary in his life and the lives of the people of Israel if they were to be recognized as the people of God. Moses was unwilling to move without the presence of God. So, too, we must be unwilling to move without first recognizing that God is with us. Moses' thought is parallel to the spiritual warfare described in James 4:7-8.

James 4:7-8

Submit therefore to God. Resist the devil and he will flee from you. Draw near to God and He will draw near to you....

— and —

Genesis 4:14 & 16

"Behold, Thou hast driven me this day from the face of the ground; and from Thy face I shall be hidden." ... Then Cain went out from the presence of the LORD....

> **Comment:** As a Christian, the most frightening situation to experience is to know that you are at odds with God and you lack the awareness of His presence.

Matthew 27:46

"ELI, ELI, LAMA SABACHTHANI?" that is, "My God, my God, why hast Thou forsaken me?"

> **Comment:** Most likely the most difficult time for Jesus on earth was when on the cross He experienced the Father withholding fellowship.

Acts 7:55-56 & 59

But being full of the Holy Spirit, he gazed intently into heaven and saw the glory of God, and Jesus standing at the right hand of God; and he said, "Behold, I see the heavens opened up and the Son of Man standing at the right hand of God...." And they went on stoning Stephen as he called upon the Lord and said, "Lord Jesus, receive my spirit!"

> **Comment:** If in the midst of being stoned Stephen could acknowledge the presence of Christ, surely we are able to do so while playing basketball or during a conflict with a family member!

Psalm 16:8-11

I have set the LORD continually before me;
> Because He is at my right hand, I will not be shaken.

Therefore, my heart is glad, and my glory rejoices;
> My flesh also will dwell securely.

For Thou wilt not abandon my soul to Sheol;
　　Neither wilt Thou allow Thy Holy One to undergo decay.
Thou wilt make known to me the path of life;
　　In Thy presence is fullness of joy;
In Thy right hand there are pleasures forever.

Comment: David practiced the presence of God. The continuous acknowledging of God's presence was a priority to him. Observe the results of David's abiding relationship with the Lord in the Psalms.

Proverbs 3:5-6

Trust in the LORD with all your heart,
　　and do not lean on your own understanding.
In all your ways acknowledge Him,
　　and He will make your paths straight.

Comment: Note the emphasis of holism (heart, understanding, all your ways) in these verses. The emphasis is on the Lord while avoiding ourselves. It is only when we deny ourselves and focus on Christ in a practical sense (interact with Him moment by moment) that He will make our paths straight. These verses remind me of that old song that says, "Turn your eyes upon Jesus and the things of the world will grow strangely dim."[4] I have found that the more I look to Jesus in the common circumstances of my life, living takes on great depth and a serene peace.

Jeremiah 9:23-24

Thus says the Lord, "Let not a wise man boast of his wisdom, and let not the mighty man boast of his might, let not a rich man boast of his riches; but let him who boasts boast of this, that he understands and knows Me, that I am the Lord who exercises lovingkindness, justice, and righteousness on earth; for I delight in these things," declares the Lord.

Comment: Here we see that what the world boasts in is contrary to the will of the LORD. But what the abiding Christian can boast in is that he understands and knows God. What an awesome thought!

Psalm 105:4

Seek the LORD and His strength;
  Seek His face continually.

Comment: Note the attitude of dependence by the use of the word continually. The more we grow in our walk with the Lord the clearer his holiness becomes and the clearer our sinfulness grips us. We as Christians can do one of two things: 1) we can turn from him in apparent independence or 2) we can turn to him in total dependence.

Matthew 14:28-31

Peter answered Him and said, "Lord, if it is You, command me to come to You on the water." And He said, "Come!" And Peter got out of the boat, and walked on the water and came toward Jesus. But seeing the wind, he became afraid, and beginning to sink, he cried out saying, "Lord, save me!" And immediately Jesus stretched out His hand and took hold of him, and said to him, "O you of little faith, why did you doubt?"

Comment: Peter was doing great until he was distracted by the wind. As soon as he took his eyes off of the Lord, he ceased to abide. Abiding means to have your gaze continually upon Christ. When we get distracted by the wind of our lives, and we begin to sink into the traps of the world and sin, we must turn to Christ and cry out for His help. If Peter did not turn away from Christ, he would never have become afraid. There is no fear of man or creation in the presence of the Creator.

John 7:37

If any man is thirsty, let him come to Me and drink.

— and —

Jeremiah 2:13

For My people have committed two evils: They have forsaken Me, The fountain of living waters, to hew for themselves cisterns, broken cisterns, that can hold no water.

Comment: These two passages remind me of many Christians. They are indeed thirsty but dig their wells into the spiritual disciplines as an end in themselves. This is like digging cisterns that cannot hold water. For the disciplines are not what we seek, just as the cisterns are not what we seek. We seek the water, the Living Water, which is Jesus and Jesus alone.

2 Corinthians 10:4-5

... for the weapons of our warfare are not of the flesh, but divinely powerful for the destruction of fortresses. We are destroying speculations and every lofty thing raised up against the knowledge of God, and we are taking every thought captive to the obedience of Christ.

Comment: A number of years ago I experienced great bitterness toward another believer because of the way he treated me and his Christian employees. I had never before experienced such prolonged bitterness. It affected my relationship with my wife, kids, school, and ministry responsibilities. I was not experiencing victory as a Christian; I was defeated. One morning God revealed to me in these two verses that victory was in Him. However, I kept the battle to myself. After this discovery whenever thoughts of this individual came into my mind I imagined reaching out and grasping them and taking them to Christ and saying, "Lord, what do you think of these?" I was victorious in Christ. I no longer lived under the bondage of an unforgiving heart and bitterness. 2 Corinthians 10:4-5 now hangs on a scroll in my office as a reminder of what I must do with every thought.

Isaiah 41:10

Do not fear, for I am with you; Do not anxiously look about you, for I am your God. I will strengthen you, surely I will help you, surely I will uphold you with My righteous right hand.

Comment: This would have been a good verse for Peter to remember when he was afraid while walking on the water (Matt. 14:28-31). Note the reason why the believer is told not to fear or be anxious—God is with him. The challenge for the Christian is to acknowledge God's presence. A similar statement can also be found in Philippians 4:6-7.

1 Thessalonians 5:16-18

Rejoice always; pray without ceasing; in everything give thanks; for this is God's will for you in Christ Jesus.

> **Comment:** Praying without ceasing is a lifestyle. We cannot be content with praying five minutes in the morning and then go throughout the day without interacting with Christ. These verses are telling us to embrace an attitude of continual, ongoing interaction with Christ—a constant dialogue.

Acts 16:6-10

And they passed through the Phrygian and Galatian region, having been forbidden by the Holy Spirit to speak the word in Asia; and when they had come to Mysia, they were trying to go into Bithynia, and the Spirit of Jesus did not permit them; and passing by Mysia, they came down to Troas. And a vision appeared to Paul in the night: a certain man of Macedonia was standing and appealing to him, and saying, 'Come over to Macedonia and help us.' And when he had seen the vision, immediately we sought to go into Macedonia, concluding that God had called us to preach the gospel to them.

> **Comment:** Paul and company were well aware of the presence of the Spirit and were able to discern His guidance. A willingness to look to Christ and an openness to do His will are necessary to be led by God. Frequently, we are too busy carrying out plans that appear to be good but miss what the Spirit desires of us.

Philippians 1:20-21

. . . according to my earnest expectation and hope, that I shall not be put to shame in anything, but that with all boldness, Christ shall even now, as always, be exalted in my body, whether by life or by death. For to me, to live is Christ, and to die is gain.

> **Comment:** The attitude Paul possessed was that all of what his life entailed was living for Christ and even dying for Christ. When we have this perspective, the stresses, struggles, and trials of life fall understandably into place.

Psalm 73:2, 17

But as for me, my feet came close to stumbling . . . .
  Until I came into the sanctuary of God . . . .

Comment: Asaph was on the verge of sinning but when he entered the presence of God (abided) he avoided sin.

Psalm 73:21-28

When my heart was embittered,
  And I was pierced within,
Then I was senseless and ignorant;
  I was like a beast before Thee.
Nevertheless I am continually with Thee;
  Thou hast taken hold of my right hand,
With Thy counsel thou wilt guide me,
  And afterward receive me to glory.
Whom have I in heaven but Thee?
  And beside Thee, I desire nothing on earth.
My flesh and my heart may fail,
  But God is the strength of my heart and my portion forever.
For, behold, those who are far from Thee will perish;
  Thou hast destroyed all those who are unfaithful to Thee.
But as for me, the nearness of God is my good;
  I have made the Lord God my refuge;
That I may tell of all Thy works.

Comment: The author, Asaph, tells us that desiring the Lord and realizing His continual presence provides all the strength and satisfaction to live life and avoid sin. We must understand this truth and live within this reality even in the midst of a world that denies God's presence and focuses on the temporal.

Proverbs 15:28

The heart of the righteous ponders how to answer,
  but the mouth of the wicked pours out evil things.

Comment: This idea of pondering (reflecting) has helped me, especially when I recognize that the Lord is there in my presence. As I am talking to another individual, I also speak to Christ. I then keep quiet and listen for His response. If He does not respond, I have learned to keep my mouth closed.

QUOTES

The following quotes give additional perspectives on abiding. Each excerpt provides another angle from which to view and understand abiding. As with the previous biblical references, each quote is accompanied by a brief comment.

Robert Coleman

"As a young boy, my father once said to me, 'Emerson where does a man go when he goes out with God?'" "I was puzzled and didn't know. When I turned to my father, I said I don't know father. Where does a man go when he goes out with God? My father had a smile on his face and said, 'Well son, does it really matter as long as you are with God?'"[5]

Comment: For Coleman, abiding includes "Trying to go out with God without running ahead, trying to look at the world from heaven's perspective." Coleman has found that, "there is little distinction between informal prayer and practicing his presence."[6] I must add, that the deeper our walk with Christ our question is no longer, "Where are we going Lord?" but rather, "Lord, show me more of You!" We become less driven to do things for him and are drawn to do things with him. The focal point no longer is activity and production but rather on the process of relating. Relationship with Christ is always followed by service (1 Timothy 1:12ff). Again, we see the Great Commission flows out of the Great Commandment. To reverse these is to attempt to do ministry in the flesh, resulting in works that will be burned up (1 Corinthians 3:10-15).

Martha Thatcher

God called David "a man after my own heart" (Acts 13:22), yet David's goal was not to become godly. Rather, he cried out, "Your face, Lord, I will seek" (Psalm 27:8). It was his focus on God that kept him from spiritual disaster: "I have set the Lord always before me. Because he is at my right hand, I will not be shaken" (Psalm 16:8).

In our right desire to be godly, we are sometimes in danger of becoming self-consumed rather than God-consumed. A friend of ours used to approach those who knew him best and ask, "Am I godly enough?" He strove to add more disciplines, more seriousness, more intensity—and, in essence, more rules—to his life to assist his progress in godliness. Years later he commented, "I wasn't really getting to know God at all. I was turned inward, consumed by my spiritual journey."

We read scores of books about the how-to's of the Christian life, and we attempt to scrutinize and reorganize our lives repeatedly. We become diligent in "spiritual" activity, yet vaguely empty inside. We grit our teeth and try earnestly to get life together, and end up evaluating ourselves in every situation.

An incredible tension develops as we create a juggling act with all the elements we are dutifully trying to maintain simultaneously. In adopting this self-focused, tense perspective we have actually been squeezed into the world's mold. We have approached the godly life with the world's "me-centered" mentality, the pressure wears us out.

A key step in reducing that pressure is to take the primary focus off ourselves and our own godliness and shift that focus to God. But how do we practice such a change in emphasis?

Remember that God is the God of all life, not just the spiritual part. He is just as relevant to our work and home and leisure situations as He is to our devotional and church activities. A series of questions will help us focus on Him increasingly in all of life:

1. How does God view this situation?
2. What are His thoughts about what should happen here?
3. Does this activity contribute to His goals?
4. In what ways is God's character at work in this?[7]

> **Comment:** Thatcher has done a superb job in not only articulating what the real problems are in many Christians' lives but she also offers some helpful and practical ways to move us in a direction of abiding.

Good News Publishers, "7 Ways to Practice God's Presence"

1. Begin each day conscious of the Lord.
2. Read God's Word.
3. Pray to the Lord.

4. Let praise be the habit of your life.
5. Praise will produce joy.
6. Learn to be quiet in the Lord's presence.
7. At the close of the day, rest in the Lord's presence.[8]

Comment: One note of caution with regard to numbers 2 and 3 in the above list. There are many Christians who diligently and routinely give regular and regimented times to reading God's word and praying. But they do these activities as an end in themselves. Their relationship with Christ is shallow. This view of the disciplines is part of the problem. When I first became a Christian I saw the spiritual disciplines as an end in themselves. You could tell I was a Christian by the fact that I had regular quiet times (QT) and Bible study. If I missed a QT, I felt guilty and knew that God was not pleased. As I grew, I began to look at the disciplines as a means to an end. In other words, these "spiritual" activities would somehow get me to God. In a very real sense I viewed them as a way to the Way. But Jesus is the Way, Truth, and Life so there must be something wrong with this perspective. The disciplines are neither an end in themselves nor a means to an end. Rather, as I turn my thoughts to Christ and recognize His presence with me, He sometimes moves me to have a QT and at other times short or extended prayer. But there are also many days that I do not do any of the disciplines. I realize that the focus is not on activity but on HIM. Just as the good Shepherd leads His sheep beside the still waters, so my good Shepherd leads me each day into activities that He has already designed for me. I am convinced that as I focus upon Him my activity will please Him.

Leighton Ford on ways to build intimacy with Christ:

1. At bedtime be at peace with the Lord (Psalm 4:4-8, Ephesians 4:26)
2. During sleep rest in the Lord (Psalm 3:5, 121:4, 127:2)
3. When sleepless, commune with the Lord (Psalm 63:6,7)
4. In the morning ask of the Lord (Psalm 5:3)
5. During the day, talk to the Lord (Psalm 25:4,5)
6. On the Sabbath, remember the Lord (Psalm 95:6-8)
7. In time of trouble wait for the Lord (Psalm 37:5-7)
8. At all times praise the Lord (Psalm 34:1)
9. Always and forever, be at home with the Lord (Psalm 27:4, 23:6).[9]

Comment: In other words, we become captivated with God. I remember when I was dating Darlene (now my wife) no one had to tell me to think about her. Every free moment I found myself thinking about her. As I come to understand all that the Lord has done for me I have less and less difficulty reflecting upon Him spontaneously.

John Piper

This is the essence of what it means to love God – to be satisfied in Him. In HIM! Loving God may include obeying all His commands; it may include believing all His Word; it may include thanking Him for all His gifts; but the essence of loving God is enjoying all He is. And it is this enjoyment of God that glorifies His worth most fully.[10]

Comment: Here Piper identifies being satisfied in God and no other thing or person. The entire book of Ecclesiastes is a testimony of the author attempting to satisfy himself in all of what the world had to offer. He concluded that the only thing in life worth doing is to fear (reverence) God and keep His commandments (Ecclesiastes 12:13). Piper, like the author of Ecclesiastes, admits satisfaction is only in God.

Jerry Bridges

The most helpful explanation I have found of what it means to abide in Christ comes from the nineteenth-century Swiss theologian Frederic Louis Godet: 'To abide in me' expresses the continual act by which the Christian sets aside everything which he might derive from his own wisdom, strength, merit, to draw all from Christ.

Paul expresses this relationship as 'living in Christ.' He says in Colossians 2:6-7, "So then, just as you received Christ Jesus as Lord, continue to live in him, rooted and built up in him, strengthened in the faith." The context of this statement is that all the wisdom and power for living the Christian life are to be found in Christ rather than in man made philosophies and moralism (see verses 2-4 and 8-10). This is what Godet is saying. We have to set aside any dependence upon our own wisdom and strength of character and draw all that we need from Christ through faith in him. This faith, of course, is expressed concretely by prayer to him. Psalm 119:33-37 is a good example of such a prayer of dependence.

This relationship is also maintained by beholding the glory of Christ in his word. In 2 Corinthians 3:18 Paul tells us that as we behold the Lord's glory, we are transformed more and more into his image. Beholding the Lord's glory in his word is more than observing his humanity in the gospels. It is observing his character, his attributes, and his will in every page of Scripture. And as we observe him, as we maintain this relationship with him through his word, we are enabled by the Holy Spirit to progressively manifest the graces of godly character.

So it is this relationship with Christ, expressed by beholding him in his word and depending upon him in prayer, that enables us to draw from him the power essential for a godly life.[11]

> **Comment:** Jerry Bridges points to the fact that beholding Jesus' glory in His word helps in the transforming process, this is indeed true. In addition, as we grow in Christ we will behold the glory of Christ in all of creation. Therefore, whether we study the Bible or study God's creation we will be able to behold His glory. We will see Him not only in the pages of Scripture but in His handiwork all around us.
>
> Bridges further explains that godly character flows from Christ. Biblically this is true and of great value. Yet, there are some who seem to go about religious activities (prayer and Bible study) to some how magically receive godly attributes. We must make the focus of our lives Christ and be satisfied in Him. If our satisfaction is Christ our character will be godly. However, if we make godly character our end we may miss an intimate relationship with Jesus our God.

Dietrich Bonhoeffer

What he really wants me to have is faith. But my faith is not necessarily tied up with riches or poverty or anything of the kind. We may be both poor and rich in the spirit. It is not important that I should have no possessions, but if I do I must keep them as though I had them not, in other words I must cultivate a spirit of inward detachment, so that my heart is not in my possessions. Jesus may have said: 'Sell thy goods,' but he meant: 'Do not let it be a matter of consequence to you that you have outward prosperity; rather keep your goods quietly, having them as if you had them not. Let not your heart be in your goods.'[12]

> **Comment:** Often the concern for our possessions radically hinders and interferes with our intimacy with Christ. We fail to embrace and deepen a re-

lationship that is abundant and eternal because of our attachment to that which is ultimately meaningless and temporal (2 Peter 3:11-12).

J. Oswald Sanders

It was love that drew John into a deeper intimacy with Jesus than the other apostles. Jesus loved them all, but John alone appropriated the title 'the disciple whom Jesus loved.' If Jesus loved John more, it was because John loved Him more. Mutual love and confidence are the keys to intimacy.

It would seem that admission to the inner circle of deepening intimacy with God is the outcome of deep desire. Only those who count such intimacy a prize worth sacrificing anything else for, are likely to attain it. If other intimacies are more desirable to us, we will not gain entry to that circle.

The place on Jesus' breast is still vacant, and open to any who are willing to pay the price of deepening intimacy. We are now, and we will be in the future, only as intimate with God as we really choose to be.[13]

Comment: Sanders emphasizes three foundational ingredients to abiding, our choice, unbroken contact, and intimate love.

William Hendriksen

In the process of bringing salvation to the hearts of men, God is ever first. By His Spirit He invades the heart of the sinner. Thus the sinner who has now become a saint has received the power to abide in Christ. The words, 'abide in Me' do not constitute a condition which man must fulfill in His own power before Christ will do His part. Far from it. It is sovereign grace from start to finish, but the responsibility of abiding in Christ is placed squarely upon man's shoulders, exactly where it belongs.[14]

Comment: Hendriksen points to a major problem which results in the lack of intimacy among many Christians today. They really do not desire an abiding relationship with Christ and therefore do not possess one. Until longing for God is greater than anything or anyone else, the Christian's intimacy with Christ will be far less than it could be.

Brother Lawrence

Brother Lawrence insisted that it is necessary to always be aware of God's presence by talking with Him throughout each day.[15]

In the beginning, Brother Lawrence declared that a little effort was needed to form the habit of continuously conversing with God, telling Him everything that was happening. But after a little careful practice, God's love refreshed him, and it all became quite easy.[16]

Our brother remarked that some people go only as far as their regular devotions, stopping there and neglecting love, which is the purpose of those devotions. This could easily be seen in their actions and explained why they possessed so little solid virtue.[17]

He said that our sanctification does not depend as much on changing our activities as it does on doing them for God rather than for ourselves.[18]

Never tire of doing even the smallest things for Him, because He isn't impressed so much with the dimensions of our work as with the love in which it is done. And we should not be discouraged if we fail in the beginning. The practice would eventually cause our efforts to become a pleasurable habit that we would do without thinking.[19]

Make a commitment never to deliberately stray from Him, to live the rest of your life in His holy presence. Don't do this in expectation of receiving heavenly comforts; simply do it out of love for Him. [20]

The only requirement is that we place our confidence entirely in God. Abandon any other concerns, including any special devotions you've undertaken simply as a means to an end. God is our "end." If we are diligently practicing His presence, we shouldn't need our former "means." We can continue our exchange of love with Him by just remaining in His holy presence. Adore Him and praise Him! There are so many ways we can thank Him. The Holy Spirit dwelling in us leads us to love God in a diversity of ways.[21]

I think the remedy for the problem (distracted from the presence of God) is to confess our faults to God and humble ourselves before Him. It isn't necessary to be too verbose in prayer, because lengthy prayers encourage wandering thoughts. Simply present yourself to God as if you were a poor man knocking on the door of a rich man, and fix your attention on His presence. If your mind wanders at times, don't be upset, because being upset will only distract you more. Allow your will to recall your attention gently to God. Such perseverance will please Him.[22]

To be with Him, we must cultivate the holy habit of thinking of Him often.

In order to know God, we must think about Him often. And once we get to know Him, we will think about Him even more often, because where our treasure is, there is our heart![23]

We can never trust this Friend of ours too much.[24]

Do not forget Him! think of Him often; adore Him ceaselessly; live and die with Him. That is the real business of a Christian; in a word, it is our profession.[25]

If we knew how much He loves us, we would always be ready to face life—both its pleasures and its troubles.[26]

In the Lord's patience, He endures our weaknesses. But just think of the price we pay by being separated from His presence![27]

We must try to converse with God in little ways while we do our work; not in memorized prayer, not trying to recite previously formed thoughts. Rather, we should purely and simply reveal our hearts as the words come to us.[28]

This doesn't mean you must leave the duties of the world forever; that would be impossible. Let prudence be your guide. But I do believe that is a common mistake of spirit-filled persons not to leave the cares of the world from time to time to praise God in their spirits and to rest in the peace of His divine presence for a few moments.[29]

In the beginning of this practice, it would not be wrong to offer short phrases that are inspired by love, such as "Lord, I am all Yours," "God of love, I love You with all my heart," or "Lord use me according to Your will." But remember to keep the mind from wandering or returning to the world. Hold your attention on God alone by exercising your will to remain in God's presence.[30]

Nicholas Herman moved to Paris and he "became a lay-brother of the Carmelite Order and took the name of Brother Lawrence.[31] He worked as a cook in a monastery and once said the following:

> I turn my little omelet in the pan for the love of God; when it is finished, if I have nothing to do, I prostrate myself on the ground and adore my God. Who gave me the grace to make it, after which I arise, more content than a king. When I cannot do anything else, it is enough for me to have lifted a straw from the earth for the love of God.[32]

During my work, I would always continue to speak to the Lord as though He were right with me, offering Him my services and thanking Him for His assistance.[33]

Brother Lawrence saw nothing but the plan of God in everything that happened to him.[34]

Everything was the same to him—every place, every job. The good brother found God everywhere, as much while he was repairing shoes as while he was praying with the community. He was in no hurry to go on retreats, because he found the same God to love and adore in his ordinary work as in the depth of the desert.[35]

Comment: Lawrence has many helpful suggestions for abiding in Christ. It seems however, that without the attitude of realizing that God is ever present with us that the normal and often required activities of life are carried out and we miss vital opportunities to commune with God and do our daily tasks for His glory. This situation describes many Christians and Christian leaders today.

Jeanne Guyon

To penetrate deeper in the experience of Jesus Christ, it is required that you begin to abandon your whole existence, giving it up to God. Let us take the daily occurrences of life as an illustration. You must utterly believe that the circumstances of your life, that is, every minute of your life, as well as the whole course of your life – anything, yes everything that happens have all come to you by His will and by His permission. You must utterly believe that everything that has happened to you is from God and is exactly what you need.[36]

... but knowing the depths of Jesus Christ is not just a method. It is a life-long attitude. It is a matter of being enveloped by God and possessed by Him.[37]

Become abandoned by simply resigning yourself to what the Lord wants, in all things, no matter what they are, where they come from, or how they affect your life.

What is abandonment? It is forgetting your past; it is leaving the future in His hands; it is devoting the present fully and completely to your Lord. Abandonment is being satisfied with the present moment, no matter what that moment contains. You are satisfied because you know that whatever that moment has, it contains—in that instant—God's eternal plan for you.[38]

Remember, you must never blame man for anything. No matter what happens, it was neither man nor circumstances that brought it. You must accept everything (except, of course, your own sinfulness) as having come from your Lord.[39]

In all your experience of Christ, it is wisest for you to stay away from any set form, or pattern, or way. Instead, be wholly given up to the leading of the Holy Spirit.[40]

The more clearly you see your true self, the clearer you also see how miserable your self nature really is; and the more you will abandon your whole being to God. Seeing that you have such a desperate need of Him, you will press toward a more intimate relationship with Him.[41]

Your external activities are those which can be seen outwardly. They have to do with, more or less, physical things. Now this you must see: There is no real goodness in them, no spiritual growth in them, and very little experience of Christ!

Of course, there is an exception: if your outward actions are a result (a by-product) of something that has taken place deep within you, then these outward actions do receive spiritual value and they do possess real goodness. But outward activities have only as much spiritual value as they receive from their source.[42]

What do I mean by this continuous inner abiding? To be continuously turned deep inside simply means that, having turned within to God – by a direct act – you have remained in His presence. You have no further need to keep turning to Christ; you already abide with Him in the chambers of your spirit. The only time you need to make a point of turning again is when your abiding is interrupted for some reason.[43]

> **Comment:** Mme. Guyon implies that we avoid a dichotomy I often see in my own life and in the lives of other Christians. We are quick to acknowledge the sovereignty of God and also His love for us; but when difficult times come our way, we do not bring the sovereignty of God and the love of God for us together. When I bring these two truths together, my awareness of God's presence is heightened. I am reminded that not only has He allowed this situation to occur but He has allowed it because He loves me.

Roy and Revel Hession

While so many Christians are content to live at a very low level, it is good that some do become concerned about their Christian lives, and it is right that they should. However, the concern arises not so much from a hunger for God, but from a longing to find an inner experience of happiness, joy, and power, and we find ourselves looking for "*it*", rather than *God* Himself.[44]

> **Comment:** The Hessions' quote reminds me of a subtle form of idolatry. It is not the joy, happiness, or power that we should pursue on earth but rather Jesus and Him alone! If power and happiness come, that is fine; even if they do not, my pursuit of God must not be conditional on what He may give to me.

To concentrate on service and activity for God may often actively thwart our attaining of the true goal, God Himself. At first sight it seems heroic to fling our lives away in the service of God and of our fellows. We feel it is bound to mean more to Him than our experience of Him. Service seems so unselfish, whereas concentrating on our walk with God seems selfish and self-centered. But it is the very reverse. The things that God is most concerned about are our coldness of heart towards Himself and our proud, unbroken natures. Christian service of itself can, and so often does, leave our self-centered nature untouched. That is why there is scarcely a church, a mission station, or a committee undertaking a special piece of service that is without an unresolved problem of personal relationships eating out its heart and thwarting its progress. This is because Christian service often gives us opportunities of leadership and position that we could not attain in the secular world, and we quickly fall into pride, self-seeking, and ambition. With those things hidden in our hearts, we have only to work alongside others, and we find resentment, hardness, criticism, jealousy, and frustration issuing from our hearts. We think we are working for God, but the test of how little of our service is for Him is revealed by our resentment or self-pity, when the actions of others, or circumstances, or ill-health take it from us![45]

> **Comment:** What the Hessions have identified is that too often many Christian leaders are calling people to experience something that they who are doing the calling are not experiencing themselves! This circumstance occurs when we focus on the Great Commission rather than the Great Commandment.

It has often been said, "The secret is in the abiding." But that is not so, for it makes the secret to reside in something we do, and this can only lead to yet another form of striving, the striving to abide. The secret surely lies in the Vine, and the blessing comes from our seeing Him as such – and as we see Him, before we know it, we are abiding![46]

> **Comment:** We must continually remind ourselves where the secret lies. The Hessions remind us that the secret is not in a thing, idea, process, or another person but only in Jesus the Vine.

METAPHORS

I have chosen to use certain metaphors to emphasize various dimensions of abiding. Sometimes the metaphor takes the form of a word or concept and at other times more of a relationship. Both are used to clarify the practical aspects of abiding. Occasionally comments follow some of the metaphors to highlight a specific point.

A Soldier

A soldier does not report to his military leader and say, "This is what I want to do today as I go about my life." Rather, he says "Sir what do you want me to do as we walk together today?"

> **Comment:** Keeping this soldier metaphor in mind, I have found that when I have long periods of not acknowledging God's presence, I usually start those days out with thoughts like "I must do this and I must get this done." But when I start and continue my day by asking, "Lord what is it that we will do today?" then I don't get stressed and I do sense His presence. I expect Him to lead me as I am practically aware of His presence.

A Child and His Father

As a young boy helped his dad build a skate board ramp, he would constantly ask, "Dad, what do you want me to do?" As the young boy completed his task, he came back to his dad and asked again, "What is it, dad, that you want me to do?" Even though the young boy did the task his dad gave him to do, the boy was constantly aware that his dad was right there working with him.

> **Comment:** Even though the routine of our daily lives is often varied we do have the ability to work in such a way that acknowledges the Lord's presence. When you finish a task simply call out to your heavenly Father, acknowledge His presence and ask for direction.

The "Jesus Nut"

There is a large nut that secures the blade of a helicopter to the main shaft. It is called a "Jesus Nut." When I asked a helicopter mechanic why the nut was called a Jesus Nut, he told me that if that nut comes off the helicopter goes down! The Jesus Nut holds the helicopter together.

Comment: If we really believe Jesus holds everything together in our lives, we would be far more apt to abide in His presence; not only when the storms of life come but also the joys.

Electric Motor

The Christian is not like an automobile with a self-contained power source; rather, he is like an electric motor that must be *constantly* connected to an outside current for its power. Our source of power is the risen Christ.[47]

White Fang

In the book *White Fang,* Jack London tells the story of an animal with that name who was half wolf, half dog. One day White Fang strayed into a hen run and killed several hens. The owner was naturally very angry. White Fang's trainer said to him, "I will guarantee that he will remain a whole afternoon in the hen run and not kill a single chicken."

The test began. Whenever the old lust to kill asserted itself, his master's voice recalled White Fang again and again, until at last the force of the impulse had spent itself as he listened to that quietly restraining voice. He finally fell asleep in the midst of the hens. When he woke up, he yawned and jumped out of the hen run. The temptation had no more power to allure. White Fang's victory over his wolf nature sprang from the restraining power of his loved master's voice. So with us. Sensitive obedience to the restraining and empowering voice of the Spirit brings victory.[48]

> **Comment:** The quote from White Fang is a healthy reminder that even though the master calls, the dog that has no desire to listen and obey will pursue his natural instincts. Christians, like White Fang, must be looking to their Master. If we truly acknowledge His presence, we will be changed and will not walk according to our flesh (the wolf part) but will walk in the Spirit and thereby manifest the Spirit's fruit.

Ulysses and the Sirens

When Ulysses and his men set out on their journey of conquest, they were warned by Circe to avoid the sirens at all costs. She told them that the sirens' voices were alluring but fatal to all who stopped to listen. The unfortunate listeners became rooted like a tree and could not tear themselves away, until they died of hunger.

"Fill your companions' ears with wax," she counseled. "If you yourself want to listen to their song, first let your men bind you securely to the mast." Ulysses heeded her advice. "If the melody beguiles me," he ordered them, "I charge you, disobey my word, and bend more strongly to your oars."

At length Ulysses heard the beautiful strains that stole into his mind, overpowered his body, and overcame his will. As the music came sweeter and sweeter, Ulysses' love for home weakened. He struggled with his shame, but as last the bewitching voices of the sirens prevailed.

"Loose me and let me stay with the sirens!" he raged. He threatened and entreated; he promised his men mountains of gold with desperate signs and gestures. His men only bound him more securely. He raged and tore at his bonds, for it was agony for him to leave the spot. But not until the last sound of music died away did they loose him. He had passed out of the zone of temptation.[49]

Comment: Figuratively speaking, sometimes putting wax in our ears is necessary to help us turn away from sin and abide. I suspect, however, that the more we abide the easier it will be to listen to Him even with no need for any secondary tools such as wax.

Jason and the Argonauts

Jason with his Argonauts set out in search of the Golden Fleece. Medea warned Jason and his men of the menace of the sirens, as they began to hear their bewitching strains. All around they could see the shore strewn with the bones of those who had succumbed to the sirens' charms. On board the boat was Orpheus, the king of minstrels.

"Let them match their songs with mine," he challenged the three maidens whom they could see, and whose silvery voices stole over the moonlit waters.

There were seagulls in long lines and shoals of fish that came to listen. The oars of Jason's heroes fell from their hypnotized hands. Their heads drooped, and their heavy eyes closed.

Then Medea cried to Orpheus, "Sing louder! Wake up these sluggards!" Orpheus struck his skillful hand over the strings of his lyre, and his voice rose like a trumpet. The music penetrated the souls of the infatuated men, and their souls thrilled. Orpheus kept on singing until his voice completely drowned the voices of the sirens. Once again the Argonauts took up their oars and Jason and his men sailed to victory. "Sing the song again, Orpheus," they cried. "We will dare and suffer to the last."[50]

Comment: We need to be weaned from the tempting music, the seductive voices and vices of today. Just as the Argonauts were revived by the music of Orpheus, the king of minstrels, even more shall we be revived and guided by Jesus, King of Kings and Lord of Lords. But we must be looking to Him, we must be captivated by His presence. Then when He speaks, we will hear and desire to do nothing but obey, not out of obligation but out of gratitude.

The Ocean and the Sun

Observe the ocean. The water in the ocean begins to evaporate. Then the vapor begins moving toward the sun. As the vapor leaves the earth, it is full of impurities; however, as it ascends, it becomes more refined and more purified. What did the vapor do? The vapor did nothing. It simply remained passive. The purifying took place as the vapor was drawn up into the heavens![51]

Comment: As Christians we would be wise to learn from the simplicity of this example. The purifying work is initiated, continues and will be completed by Christ. Our role is to abide in Him.

A Frightened Child

What does a little child do when he sees something that frightens him or confuses him? He doesn't stand there and try to fight the thing. He will, in fact, hardly look at the thing that frightens him. Rather, the child will quickly *run* into the arms of his mother.[52]

Comment: The idea of running to God is very healthy. The more we run to Him the less running we will do. As we continue to abide in Him, we will not have to run to Him because we will know He is with us.

Tracking God

Don Bartel, a Navigator missionary, once told me of some ideas he had learned from an expert in the field of tracking animals. If you are tracking an animal, what you really want to see is the animal! However, unless you have the opportunity to see the animal outright you must learn the skills of tracking in order to see an animal face to face. The following is a brief list of four ideas in regard to tracking:

1. *Territory* – If you are looking for a lion, the idea of territory consists of knowing where lions live and roam. You will not find too many lions at the North Pole. You need to study their living and eating habits.

2. *Secondary Sighting* – This consists of recognizing the impact of an animal on its surroundings. If while tracking a lion, you enter an area that is always populated by zebras but find no zebras in sight except for a half eaten carcass, you may conclude that a lion is in the area.

3. *Primary Sighting* – While investigating the soil surrounding the zebra's carcass you discover a significant primary sighting of paw prints. As you grow in the study and pursuit of the lion, you will learn where to look for a second paw print if only one is initially visible because you are aware of the walking characteristics of a lion. As your experiential knowledge increases about tracking a lion, weight distribution becomes a factor. You will be able to tell whether the lion was running, walking, or standing. If it was standing, you will be able to tell whether it was looking to the left, right, or to the rear.

4. *Direct Sighting* – Now that you have discovered his domain, evidenced both his presence and paw prints you want to have a direct sighting, i.e., see him face to face. But when you come face to face with a lion and there are no bars between him and you, you can become very frightened![53]

   Comment: Tracking God can be very similar to tracking a lion. Tracking God is an attractive idea to many people. But they often turn away from the path of God because all they want is a direct sighting. However, most of us will not experience a direct sighting this side of death; but, there are many territorial, secondary, and primary evidences of God that are significant motivators to the Christian in his relationship to God. Territorial indications must be considered while pursuing God. The world is under the dominion of Satan; therefore, are there any indications that the Holy Spirit is taking back His territory? Secondary influences [impact upon surroundings] must also be considered. Are individuals living a life of unity and developing and employing their spiritual gifts? Primary sightings might be equated with the demonstration of the miracles of God. But none of these is a direct sighting of God; and, after all, that is what we want! We must remember that sometimes even God's footprints are difficult to see (Psalm 77:19).

Abiding in Christ is learning how to track God, sensing His presence everywhere, seeing Him work in both the believer and nonbeliever's lives, and acknowledging the miracle He is working out in every aspect of our lives. We will see Him one day face to face but until that time we must trust and depend upon Him for everything.

Therefore, anytime we find ourselves being anxious or fearful at that moment we are attempting to be or do something God has either not designed us for or we are not abiding in Him. Scripture clearly indicates that we have been designed for His glory and as we follow Him, He will lead us into service (1 Timothy 1:12-14) which He has not only prepared before hand for us (Ephesians 2:10) but also has equipped us to do (Hebrews 13:21).

PRINCIPLES OF ABIDING

The following principles have been placed under one of the following categories indicating the focus of each principle:

> Our Position in regard to Christ
>> The Practice of abiding
>>> The Result of abiding

Positional

1. The law of the Spirit has set us free from the law of sin and death (Romans 8:2).
2. The most perfect union with God is the actual presence of God.[54]
3. God has made us solely for Himself.

Practical

1. Focus on God, not on being godly or serving God. The more you focus on God the more godliness and service will be seen in your life.
2. Take your thoughts captive to Christ (2 Corinthians 10:5).
3. Trust Christ for everything, even the little things of life.
4. As you go through the commonness of your daily life, ask Christ questions and then listen.
5. Abiding is your responsibility.
6. Abiding is the only way for the fruit of the Spirit to be exhibited in your life.
7. A focus on self, abiding or anything else will hinder intimacy with Christ. Christ is the focus.
8. Abiding is reciprocal (John 15:7).
9. We should be considerate of God in everything we do and say.[55]
10. The most holy and necessary practice in our lives is the presence of God.[56]
11. Immaturity considers the Lord Jesus a helper. Maturity knows Him to be life itself.
12. I have discovered that the ability to commune and truly abide in Christ is not found outside of myself. For if Christ dwells within me, then I must turn inwardly to abide.
13. The more you experience Christ in your "whole-person" (windows and door), the more you will come to know Christ.
14. God gives us the cross, and then the cross gives us God.[57]
15. To concentrate on service and activity for God may actively thwart our attaining of the true goal, God Himself.[58]

16. The acknowledgment of need and the confession of sin, therefore, is always the first step in seeing Jesus.[59]

17. That which does not anticipate and have an answer for the sin that comes can never be the way for the Christian.[60]

18. The Way is not Bible study, Scripture memory, witnessing, fellowship but only Jesus!

19. You are unable to produce the fruit of the Spirit in the flesh.

20. According to 1 Thessalonians 4:16-17 when Christ comes to take us home it is at that time we will experience the presence of the Lord *continually.* Here on earth experiencing the presence of Christ will continue to grow but there will be times that His presence will seem more of a reality than other times. Nonetheless, we thank God we have the privilege to experience Christ now and the joy of His presence.

Result

1. Fruit of the Spirit is the evidence of abiding (John 15:8).

2. Abundant joy is the result of a lifestyle of abiding (John 15:11).

Summary

J.I. Packer said, "The width of our knowledge about Him is no gauge of the depth of our knowledge of Him."[61] Packer identifies the focal point of the Christian life—lived-out Christianity, a life of experiencing Christ throughout the everyday joy and struggles of life. In his song "Experience," Charlie Peacock highlights this truth:

> There is a difference,
> A qualitative difference,
> between what I know as a fact
> and what I know as truth.
> The facts of theology
> can be altogether cold;
> While true in every way,
> they alone can't change me.
> Truth is creative, transforming
> and alive –
> it's the truth that keeps me humble,
> saved and set free.
> We can only possess what we experience;

Truth to be understood must be lived.[62]

Shadrach, Meshach, and Abednego had the opportunity to live out their beliefs in a fiery furnace. They gave themselves fully to God for him to do as he chose. It is interesting to note that in Daniel 3:21 we learn that Daniel's three friends were tied up with a rope. Yet, in verse 25 they were loosed from their bonds, for they were abiding with Christ in the furnace. Because of Jesus' finished work on the cross, abiding in Him loosens people from the oppressive effects of the limitations of the world, the flesh, the Devil, and sin (Romans 6:11-12). We Christians need to realize that positionally we have been freed from all bondage, but practically we must abide with Christ to live in freedom. Christ died for our sins; we must die to our sins. Abiding is the only way to die to our sins. If we abide in Christ we will be dead to sins' influence but if we abide in our flesh sins' magnetism will be very strong. A.W. Tozer wisely stated:

Everything in the New Testament accords with this Old Testament picture. Ransomed men need no longer pause in fear to enter the Holy of Holies. God wills that we should push on into His Presence and live our whole life there. This is to be known to us in conscious experience. It is more than a doctrine to be held, it is a life to be enjoyed every moment of every day.[63]

Early in our spiritual journey our relationships with Christ, (our "spirituality"), tends to be measured more by what we do. Do we act the right way; do we avoid bad activities? Our emphasis is on the external. As we grow in Him, we tend to view life more from the inside out. Our focus will be on the process of life; i.e., on being rather than on a product or production of life. Our gaze is one of intimacy and union while serving God out of gratitude.

Activity is still occurring for the abiding Christian. Rather than we being the stimulus and response, God is the stimulus. God is the one drawing us unto Himself, and we respond to the drawing power of His love. Each of us will probably abide and respond to Him differently. Some will feel the Lord's presence more than others. This is understandable and natural but feelings are not necessarily our guide for abiding.

Be careful how you train new and young believers. Do not burden them with a host of activity, no matter how "spiritual." Rather, lead them to God by helping them turn within to Christ and enjoy His presence. Teach them to seek God within their own heart.

There are some who make clear distinctions between spiritual activities and anything else. To these people, car mechanics would not be a spiritual activity but one that is probably necessary. Some would say that car mechanics is a spiritual activity and that they do it *for* Jesus. But I want to affirm that car mechanics is certainly a spiritual activity and I would recommend doing it *with* Jesus. The key to spiritual maturity is not outward activity but a heart for God.

Too often believers act as though they are human doings rather than human beings. Remember, the issue is not doing things for Christ but with Him. This perspective allows me to view my intimate relationship with Christ as primary over service.

Do you recall how the Lord rebuked the Ephesian church in Revelation 2:1-7? He was pleased with their perseverance for His name's sake against the evil men and false teachers. Yet He said, "But I have this against you, that you have left your first love." We must help believers develop a heart and a love for God without seeing forms and rules as an end in themselves or a means to an end. We want them to realize that self effort must continue to cease and the volitional window will become more passive in Christ's presence. This, of course, is a process and will take time. Their growth in Christ can be facilitated if we help them early on avoid these pitfalls and see Christ as the end. Often growth built upon rules and forms is a house built upon sand. Remember, when they received Christ, they received the ultimate in life; there is nothing more except experiencing His presence. Help them to enjoy His presence – the internal adventure – and they will serve Him fully!

Notes

[1]Produced by Chicago Multi-Media.

[2]Margaret Becker's song "No Other" (co-written with Donna Douglas) captures this type of commitment beautifully.

> All the evidence is in – all the truth's been told
>
> There's nothing left I need to see – 'cause I'm already sold
>
> > I've seen the healing touch of Your hand – bring broken dreams to life
>
> No one can love me any more than You, so I make this vow tonight
>
> *Chorus*
>
> *(There'll be)*
>
> *No other God before You. No other love above You.*
>
> *No other dream in my heart – than what You've begun.*
>
> *Before You there will be – no other one.*

I cannot see where life will take me – there's still so far to go.

But this one thing I've come to realize – You're all I need to know.

>Against the frailty of my humanness – with everything I am I promise this

>*Chorus*

Oh Precious Love that found me

All that You are is all I need.

>*Chorus*

Recorded on *Along the Road,* Susan Ashton, Margaret Becker, Christine Denté (Brentwood: Sparrow Corporation, 1994).

[3] *Chariots of Fire* (Warner Brothers).

[4] "Turn Your Eyes Upon Jesus" Text and Music by Helen H. Lemmel (1922); renewal 1950 by H.H. Lemmel, assigned to Singspiration, Inc.

[5] Author's conversation with Robert Coleman.

[6] Ibid.

[7] Martha Thatcher, "The Inward Battle For Purity," Navlog, Vol. 47, N. 4 (August 1986).

[8] Good News Publishers, *Ways to Practice God's Presence* (Westchester: Good News Publishers.

[9] Leighton Ford, *Nine Ways To Build Intimacy With Christ* (6230 Fairview Road, Suite 300, Charlotte, NC 28210).

[10] Adapted from, "Are You Satisfied with God?," *TableTalk* (Ligonier Ministries).

[11] Jerry Bridges, *The Practice of Godliness* (Colorado Springs: NavPress, 1988), p. 74. Bridges' quote is from Frederic Louis Godet, *Commentary on John's Gospel* (Grand Rapids: Kregel Publications, 1978), p. 855.

[12] Dietrich Bonhoeffer, *The Cost of Discipleship* (London: SCM Press Ltd., 1959; reprinted New York: Touchstone Books, Simon & Schuster Inc., 1995), p. 88.

[13] J. Oswald Sanders, *Enjoying Intimacy With God* (Chicago: Moody Press, 1980), p. 69. He also remarks: "Abiding in Christ is, of course, possible only to real Christians. It means keeping unbroken contact with Christ in a union of intimate love" (p. 18).

[14] William Hendriksen, *Galatians* (Grand Rapids: Baker Book House, 1968), p. 52.

[15] Brother Lawrence, *The Practice of the Presence Of God* (Springdale: Whitaker House, 1982), p. 8.

[16] Ibid., p. 11.

[17] Ibid., pp. 17-18.

[18] Ibid., p. 20.

[19] Ibid., p. 21.

[20] Ibid., p. 30.

[21] Ibid., p. 32.

[22] Ibid., p. 43.

[23] Ibid., p. 46.

[24] Ibid., p. 47.

[25] Ibid., p. 48.

[26] Ibid., p. 53.

[27] Ibid., p. 54.

[28] Ibid., p. 59.

[29] Ibid., p. 60.

[30] Ibid., p. 70.

[31] Ibid., p. 78.

[32] Ibid., p. 81.

[33] Ibid., p. 82.

[34] Ibid., p. 89.

[35] Ibid., p. 90.

[36] Jeanne Guyon, *Experiencing The Depths Of Jesus Christ* (Gardiner: Christian Books), p. 32.

[37] Ibid., pp. 32-33.

[38] Ibid., p. 35.

[39] Ibid., p. 36.

[40] Ibid., p. 80.

[41] Ibid., p. 84.

[42] Ibid., p. 107.

[43] Ibid., p. 110.

[44] Roy and Revel Hession, *We Would See Jesus* (Fort Washington: Christian Literature Crusade, n.d.), p. 11.

[45] Ibid., pp. 14-15.

[46] Ibid., p. 95.

[47] Bridges, p. 75.

[48] Sanders, p. 90.

[49] Ibid.

[50] Ibid.

[51] Guyon, pp. 53-54.

[52] Ibid., p. 85.

[53] Private conversation with author.

[54] Lawrence, p. 65.

[55] Ibid., p. 57.

[56] Ibid., p. 59.

[57] Guyon, p. 38.

[58] Hession, p. 14.

[59] Ibid, p. 23.

[60] Ibid, p. 65.

[61] J.I. Packer, *Knowing God* (Downers Grove: InterVarsity Press, 1973), p. 34.

[62] Charlie Peacock, *The Secret of Time* (Brentwood: Sparrow Corporation).

[63] A.W. Tozer, *The Pursuit of God* (Harrisburg: Christian Publications, Inc., 1948), pp. 36-37.

Review – Section Two

In this section we encountered a glimmer of light found in the proclaimed work of Jesus in the Gospel of Luke and are encouraged that Jesus not only understood that our problem touched all of who and what we are, but that He also provided a solution which is holistic as well. The primary avenue for being set free from our bondage in sin is truth, specifically in knowing the truth as found in Christ and through abiding in Christ. We also were shown how the holiness of God is the foundation for understanding our personal freedom in Christ. Acknowledging and living in the presence of God must be applied in discipling relationships or else we fundamentally undermine the saving work of Christ in life.

As rational, physical, moral, volitional, emotional, and relational beings we saw how truth and The Truth, Jesus Christ, sets us free. We encountered God in His awesome holiness, and saw the reality that as we experience His holiness change becomes possible in the practical everyday sense.

Both the Bible and the experience of others teaches and shows us that the intimacy, joy, and abundant life promised by Christ can be realities now in the present not something to look forward to in the future. Even so, we do look to that time when we shall be with him face-to-face for then:

"we shall be like Him, because we shall see Him as He is"
— 1 John 3:2 —

What it means to abide in Christ and the practical implications of acknowledging and living in the presence of God were shown to be the only way for us to experience:

the life we want in Christ.

SECTION THREE

The Process — Growth

CHAPTER 8

Understanding Roles: The Builder
and the Apprentice

"And He, when He comes, will convict the world concerning sin, and righteousness, and judgment; concerning sin, because they do not believe in Me; and concerning righteousness, because I go to the Father, and you no longer behold Me; and concerning judgment, because the ruler of this world has been judged."
— John 16:8-11 —

How often have you attempted to do something that was not your job only to have the whole situation backfire? For me the times were many! There is a clear example of this in 1 Samuel 13:11-14:

> ... Samuel said, "What have you done?" And Saul said, "Because I saw that the people were scattering from me, and that you did not come within the appointed days, and that the Philistines were assembling at Michmash, therefore I said, 'Now the Philistines will come down against me at Gilgal, and I have not asked the favor of the Lord.' So I forced myself and offered the burnt offering." And Samuel said to Saul, "You have acted foolishly; you have not kept the commandment of the Lord your God, which He commanded you, for now the Lord would have established your kingdom over Israel forever. But now your kingdom shall not endure. The Lord has sought out for Himself a man after His own heart, and the Lord has appointed him as ruler over His people, because you have not kept what the Lord commanded you."

King Saul made a serious mistake. He assumed the role of a priest and performed priestly duties. But who can really blame him? Think about it. What would you have done? Let me paraphrase his response to Samuel's question "What have you done?" to sharpen Saul's apparent dilemma and thinking on the problem. Samuel, you didn't come when you said you would, the people were starting to desert me, and, to make matters worse, our arch enemy the Philistines were organizing to attack us. As any clear thinking person can see, things were not looking good. I'm the king and the people look to me to lead and guide them. I needed to keep them together so we could fight the Philistines. Since we always offer a burnt offering to the Lord to guarantee his favor and you weren't here to do it, I did the next best and most logical thing (even though I knew I shouldn't have): I forced myself to offer the burnt offering.

Saul's argument at first glance certainly seems reasonable in light of the situation. But neither God nor Samuel was pleased at Saul's seeming rational decision. Why? Because Saul was the king not a priest and was unqualified and prohibited from performing in the place of a priest. Because Saul, *thinking things were up to him,* presumed to fulfill a role limited to the priesthood. Even though circumstances appeared bleak and disaster seemed imminent, God was still in control. Saul acted out of fear, presumption, and unbelief rather than from faith, reliance, and trust. As can be seen from the rest of the passage, Saul paid dearly for his decision.

Through my own poor decisions and by observing similar actions of other Christians, I have discovered that many of us have been attempting to assume the role of the Holy Spirit in trying to influence non-Christians to seek God and follow Christ. Like Saul, we have made a terrible error. God is not pleased when we do this nor is His kingdom advanced. The purpose of this chapter is to help clarify the role of the Holy Spirit and the role of the Christian in reference to influencing non-Christians. Understanding these roles and their differences will help free us from attempting to do what we are not qualified or even able to do. By identifying what we as Christians have been called to do from that of the Holy Spirit, we can understand our role, work in harmony with the Holy Spirit in His convicting ministry, and stop hindering His ministry in and to the world.

Convicting the World Concerning Sin

It is probably safe to say that most people in the world do not believe in Jesus. Jesus said that one of the reasons He was sending the Holy Spirit into the world was to "convict the world concerning sin, and righteousness, and judgment" (John 16:8). When people become believers, they become much more sensitive to what Jesus says about their sin due to their acknowledgment of who Christ is and of their growing intimacy with Him and His holiness. The Holy Spirit's task is to convict[1] both Christians as well as non-Christians, who have no such relationship to Christ, of their sin and heart condition. We could say that the Spirit of God is the ultimate or paramount prosecuting attorney.[2] Every man, woman, and child is directly faced with the fact of their personal sin. Without this work of the Holy Spirit, non-Christians would live in ignorance of their lost condition and that they are on the course to condemnation. Christians would flounder along the path of righteousness as they struggled to discern right from wrong and good from evil.

As we live and minister to others we need to remember that the motivation behind the Holy Spirit's convicting work is the salvation of the non-Christian, the sanctification of the Christian, and the glorification of Christ and God the Father. The Spirit's labor is not conviction as an end in itself, but is rather the means to our salvation and developing intimacy with Christ.

The important point is this: even though it may seem to us that the Holy Spirit does not appear to be working very effectively at times, let us trust Him that He is doing His job in His way and in His time while we focus on knowing Christ and living in His presence serving others in the anticipation and hope that they might come to know Christ too.

Convicting the World Concerning Righteousness

Most, if not all, people in some way tend to rationalize their sinful acts by attempting to justify them. Many deny committing any sinful acts whatsoever while others, being somewhat more honest, say, "Yes, I have done wrong things, but never maliciously." There are even others who admit, at least to themselves and sometimes to others, "Yes, I have intentionally committed some cruel acts." Yet even though there appears to be varying levels of honesty in regard to sinful behavior, still we humans at our core tend to rationalize and justify our sinful behavior. We do this repeatedly for selfish and protective purposes in order to appear, if only in our own minds that we are really okay (after all, our own individual standards are the ones which really count!). After all, if there is a God, He will certainly understand what we have done and see that we are indeed righteous.

The fact is, however, that *God does not excuse or overlook our sin:* "all our righteous deeds are like a filthy garment" (Isaiah 64:6). God will not understand, God will not overlook: God will do nothing less then condemn our sin. The Holy Spirit's task is to reveal that our acts of righteousness are nothing but garbage to God. God is righteous and holy, and apart from this awareness of God's character, we would have no understanding of our personal inadequacy to be holy and righteous. Establishing and upholding God's absolute standards in the minds of humanity is a primary responsibility of the Holy Spirit. Through His sinless life, Jesus convicted others of their empty righteousness. The Holy Spirit continues Jesus' work through his convicting influence enabling the Christian to live a life of love and enabling the non-Christian to come to know Christ.

Convicting the World Concerning Judgment

Earlier we discovered that part of Jesus' job description entailed giving sight to the blind (Luke 4). Non-Christians are spiritually blind and live in a world filled with the darkness of the Evil One, Satan. They accept the evil of the world as normal – it is the status quo. They do not see the divergence between light and darkness, the disparity between them which becomes ever greater and greater to the growing Christian.

Whenever we realize that our sinful lifestyle is at odds with the righteous character of God, conviction of judgment is the result. With Christ's obedience on the cross, we see Satan's rebellious self-will and ours come under God's judgment.

While being crucified, Jesus cried out to the Father and asked God to forgive the soldiers who were crucifying Him (Luke 23:34). Those soldiers were blind to their deeds; they needed to be enlightened. Those Roman warriors believed they were doing their jobs. And they were. Blindly carrying out the deeds of darkness, they submitted to the wishes of the Father of Darkness. Those soldiers, and many in the world today, incorrectly judged Jesus as guilty. But when Jesus rose from the dead, the Strongman (Satan, the Devil) was defeated and rendered impotent. So the Holy Spirit was sent and even now moves graciously among us, the ignorant and lost, revealing to us that our estimation of Jesus, the loving God of humanity, is dreadfully, disastrously, destructively, deliberately wrong. The Spirit enlightens and reveals that Jesus openly and willingly waits for us to turn from a life in darkness to the life of light. And for those who are so transformed, they are also transferred from the dominion of darkness and receive residence in the kingdom of God's love and light.[3]

Light Bearers

"You are the light of the world. A city set on a hill cannot be hidden. Nor do men light a lamp, and put it under the peck-measure, but on the lampstand, and it gives light to all who are in the house. Let your light shine before men in such a way that they may see your good works, and glorify your Father who is in heaven." (Matthew 5:14-16)

When I was growing up in the coal regions of Pennsylvania, my parents and I participated in a tour of a coal mine. I really enjoyed the experience and can remember the coolness of the mine and the lights lining its walls. After we had walked a considerable distance into the mine shaft, the miner leading the tour shut off all the lights.

While people were making all kinds of remarks about how dark it was, I attempted to see my hand as I held it six inches from my face. I could not see a thing. So I waited for my eyes to adjust. Nothing! I could not even see a faint outline of my hand. Suddenly, the coal miner flicked on the light that was attached to his hardhat. Then he described what coal miners look for in the mine shaft and pointed to a vein of coal running along the wall. The problem was that my eyes had adjusted to the darkness. The miner stood across from me and while pointing out the coal, the light of his helmet shined directly into my eyes. It really hurt! As might be expected, I did not see what the miner was attempting to show me. During his talk he moved along side of me so that his light was directed onto the wall of the mine and not into my eyes. Suddenly I could clearly see the vein of coal. The coal had been there all the time, but I needed light to be shed upon it (not into my eyes!) so I could see what was once hidden in the darkness.

This story of my boyhood experience is a dim reflection, a mere shadow, of what is happening among many well-intentioned Christians working and ministering today. These Christians recognize that they are God's lights, but how their light is to be shed needs direction. Many Christians seem content to stand across from non-Christians and hurl light into eyes accustomed to darkness. Then they wonder why non-Christians do not see what the light reveals or do not understand the light shined upon them. Usually the non-Christian dismisses the Christian and/or the light as irrelevant, and sometimes they hurl back abuse, cover their eyes in shock, and seek the familiar comfort of the darkness and dark places. Some Christians interpret the abuse as persecution and joyfully chalk such incidents up as part of being an obedient Christian and of suffering righteously for Christ. In reality, hurling light beams only further damages non-Christians' views of Christ and Christianity. Our job is not to convict but to testify to and persuade others of the truth of the gospel.[4] The Holy Spirit is quite capable of performing the necessary heart surgery of conviction. This does not mean the Holy Spirit does not use us in the convicting process, because He does. But our role is to come alongside non-Christians in loving, personal, relevant relationships so that they may see what is hidden in darkness. We need to learn how to develop meaningful and authentic relationships with others so they can see the reality and relevance of the truths of Scripture working and operating in our lives. Remember, the truth does exist apart from the non-Christian's acknowledgment. Our role is to work alongside the Holy Spirit in His convicting and illuminating work by praying and developing relationships that may lead to significant discussions about the truth of Scripture.

Still we often engage in ministry attempting to produce supernatural fruit in someone else's life. The problem is that we cannot do this, no one can except the Holy Spirit. The fruit of the Spirit is just that, the fruit of the Holy Spirit. His fruit is seen in our lives when we abide in Christ and take heed to the Holy Spirit's direction (John 14:16-22, 15:1-17; Galatians 5:16-25). Abiding is a choice on every Christian's part, fruit bearing is a result of abiding and is a supernatural work on God's part. Many Christians, even seminary students, are being trained in strategies that are directed at producing supernatural fruit in their own lives and the lives of others by human means. Producing supernatural fruit by our own power or efforts will never happen. Even Jesus said that His work was done in and by the Spirit (Luke 4:18).

One healthy perspective that helps keep me from assuming the Holy Spirit's role is to remind myself that God knows the people: He knew them before they were in their mother's wombs (Psalm 139:13-16, Jeremiah 1:5, Ephesians 1:3-6). He knows all about them: what they like and do not like, what they find attractive and what they avoid (Psalm 139). Our involvement with people will be limited, but with a proper motive it can be used by God to draw them closer to Him. God was involved in their lives long before we came into the picture and He will continue to work in their lives long after we are gone from their lives.

To help clarify what our role as light in the world is, the nature of light is examined so we can consider how our being lights can be applied as we live among non-Christians.

The Nature of Light

Optics, the science of the behavior of light, is a complex area of study yet very fascinating. I remember sitting in a high school science class and learning that light travels at the speed of 186,282 miles per second or 5.8 trillion miles per year. That is fast; very fast. Light is the fastest thing known to us. But light has other characteristics than speed. For instance, light makes no sound that we can hear, but it can be felt. Light banishes darkness. Light's intensity increases as we move closer to its source and overexposure to light will burn.

Photons, tiny bundles of energy released by atoms, are critical components to the making of light. Photons that contain varying amounts of energy form different colors of light. White light is a combination of photons that cover the *whole range* of visible light. So white light is made up of all the colors of light.[5] Visible light consists of seven different wavelengths: red, orange, yellow, green, blue, indigo, and violet. A ray of sunlight contains all seven wavelengths. When we observe light, we are actually seeing the different wavelengths of light as different colors.[6]

When a ray of light encounters an object, one of three things happen: 1) the light may be *reflected*, thrown back and away from the object; 2) the ray may be *refracted*, pass into the object and become bent or distorted; or 3) the light may be *absorbed*, consumed or assimilated by the object. The way different objects reflect, refract, or absorb a ray of light gives the objects the individual colors that we see.[7] Light is what makes up the color spectrum.

When we see a white wedding gown, the material of the gown is *reflecting* the entire color spectrum. When we observe the blue shirt of a bridegroom, the material of the shirt is *absorbing* all of the colors of white light except it reflects that combination of light waves that we call blue. When we see the black slacks of a groom's tuxedo, the pants material is absorbing all of the colors of the light spectrum.

The relationship between light and objects is typically described by three terms: opaque, translucent, and transparent. Opaque describes an object that does not permit light to pass through it. Translucent describes an object that light can pass through, but the light is partial or distorted. In both of these cases we end up seeing the object instead of having a clear view of the light. Transparent describes an object where light passes freely through it resulting in our seeing the light unhindered and undistorted by the object.

With these few facts about light and objects, let us consider our role as light in a world filled with darkness.

Absorbers, Refractors, or Reflectors? Opaque, Translucent, or Transparent?

Using light as our model, we can distinguish three types of people. We are answering the question, "Who are the absorbers, who are the refractors, and who are the reflectors of light in the world?"

Absorbers are non-Christians: they totally absorb the light of the truth of the gospel shined upon them causing or resulting in no difference to themselves or to those around them. There is no supernatural life or fruit seen in their lives, and there can be none for they are spiritually dead. Instead of reflecting the light and glory of Christ, they remain self-centered and lost in their sin (Ephesians 2).

Refractors are those Christians who continue to live in their sins and have not chosen to die to self and to live for Christ (Luke 9:23-25). Their lives are bent and distorted and they give a distorted and bent witness. When a pencil is placed into a glass of water, the water refracts the light and the pencil appears to be broken. In reality, the pencil is straight but the water is giving a misrepresentation of what the pencil is really like. Even so Christians can distort and even give a broken view of Christ, the Christian life, and the reality of the gospel.

It is important to highlight that Christ lives within Christians, and as we deny self by abiding in Him, He shines through our lives from the inside out. It is the obedient Christian who totally reflects the life of Christ just as a mirror reflects light. Light reflected from a smooth surface, such as a mirror, bounces back without spreading out. But light reflected from a rough surface, such as a piece of paper spreads out. A mirror thus forms a sharp image of the light it reflects, and paper forms no image at all.[8]

When the light of Christ shines on the Christian, people do not see so much the Christian as they see Christ's light reflected by the Christian. Reflectors are those Christians who are constantly abiding in Christ and obeying His word. We are called to be reflectors not refractors or absorbers of the light.

To put it another way, consider how light moves through objects. *Opaque:* no light. *Translucent:* some distorted light. *Transparent:* clear light. The problem for non-Christians is the opaqueness of their lives apart from Christ. The problem for Christians is the translucent qualities of their lives when they are not abiding in Christ. We still have problems with our old natures, which tend to be self-absorbing and hinder the reflecting process. But when a person abides in Christ, the self-absorbing qualities disappear and Christ is seen clearly. We are called to be transparent not translucent or opaque bearers of the light.

Sin, Light, and Sanctification

Since our whole-person was tainted by sin before we became Christians, we were like a piece of paper stained dark losing its reflecting ability. Even though we have been made in the image of God, we nevertheless lived in darkness due to our self-absorption of personal sin. Darkness was trapped inside and light absorbed. There was no reflection and no sight. It is impossible to change darkness and still have darkness; the non-reflective characteristics must be eliminated by creating a reflective substance. The process of becoming a smooth, silvery surface for the light of Christ to reflect off involves God revealing our sinfulness through the struggles of our daily life experiences.

Consider the painstaking process a silversmith uses while refining silver. Unrefined silver is melted in a giant pot. As the heat increases, various impurities rise to the surface. The silversmith skims them off the surface and turns the heat up. Then he repeats the process. This cycle continues until the silversmith sees his own reflection in the silver inside the pot. Then he knows that the silver has been thoroughly purified. Christ is the Great Silversmith of our sanctification. Over and over He turns up the heat in our lives, and as we abide in Christ and the impurities of our sin rise to the surface, and as we confess our sins, He stretches out His holy hand and reaches down to remove them from our lives. Then He repeats the process. This purifying and cleansing process continues until we can brilliantly reflect a clear image of Christ.

All Christians at times refract and distort the image of God (2 Peter 1:9). When we abide in our sinful humanity and not in Christ, we refract a distorted view of Christ. More than that, in actuality we are reflecting broken fellowship with Christ. We need to be mirrors of Christ and no one else. A mirror is a piece of glass covered with silver paint resulting in the reflection of anyone who stands in front of it. A Christian is a sinful person covered by the blood of Christ. The blood of Christ washes our darkness away and results in our ability to reflect the image of Christ. As we abide in the presence of Christ, Jesus is *naturally* reflected. Sanctification is a process of moving from a darkened state of life towards a life of pure white light. We need to stop living for our darkened selves and live the light of Christ. Just as the color white is a reflection of all that light is, the abiding Christian reflects all that Christ is. As we move from immaturity to maturity in Christ, the Lord continues to gradually cleanse our lives so that they reflect the totality of pure light (John 3:21).

Reflecting the Light of Jesus

Since our redemption, we have been called to reflect the image of God like highly polished mirrors: "But we all, with unveiled face beholding as in a mirror the glory of the Lord, are being transformed into the same image from glory to glory, just as from the Lord, the Spirit" (2 Corinthians 3:18). As we develop a closer walk with Christ, we become more like Jesus. In a very real sense, we begin to reflect His glory to those around us. This is why we cannot help but be changed as we live in and acknowledge the presence of Christ. The changes that take place through the abiding process are only done through the Spirit of God and as this process continues we reflect God's glory to the world.

An example of this process is seen in the life of Moses. In Exodus 34:29-35 we are told that Moses' face actually shined because he had been abiding in the presence of God. *We become like the things or people we are around.* In this case Moses was in the presence of pure light, the source of all light. *No one comes into the presence of God and remains unchanged.* Moses physically reflected a portion of the Lord's glory. Moses experienced a very close encounter with the Lord God. The closer the reflector gets to light the more intense the reflection becomes. The Israelites begged Moses to cover his face for they were afraid of God's glory; therefore Moses wore a veil over his face. The type of glory that Moses reflected when he descended from Mount Sinai diminished over time, but he kept on the veil even though the glory had diminished (Exodus 34:29-35; 2 Corinthians 3:7-18). One might ask whether he stopped abiding in the presence of God. Moses, under the old covenant, did not have the privilege that we have under the new covenant. We have the opportunity to behold God's glory continually. We do not have to come down off the mountain. Our reflection of His glory does not need to diminish or cease. But it will if we cease to abide. The plan of God is that we progressively increase in a reflective lifestyle until we exchange the mirror of our earthly body for a glorified body like that of Christ (Philippians 3:21; 1 Corinthians 15; 1 John 3:2).

We are called to be light in a dark world, to reflect the light of God, revealing what is hidden: "For God who said, 'Light shall shine out of darkness,' is the One who has shone in our hearts to give the light of the knowledge of the glory of God in the face of Christ" (2 Corinthians 4:6). In this text, Paul describes the enabling power which stimulated him to promote the kingdom of God. Paul described not only the results of the light of Christ in his life but also in the life of all Christians. When the light of Christ enters our lives, as with Paul, it dispels darkness and we begin to see what once was hidden and misunderstood.

Light is not only the opposite of darkness, but in Scripture is synonymous with truth, wisdom, and purity. The more we abide in Christ, practicing the presence of God, the more we naturally reflect him: "For you were formerly darkness, but now you are light in the Lord; walk as children of light. . . . And do not participate in the unfruitful deeds of darkness, but instead even expose them" (Ephesians 5:8,11). The purpose of the light of God's word is to reveal and expose what is hidden in darkness, not to blind. The non-Christian is already spiritually blind. The challenge for "light bearers" is the same as for the coal miner: if we want people to see what is hidden in darkness, we need to get in a position alongside others in authentic friendship so that when the light of our lives naturally shines, those around us will see the reality and relevance of Christ to life. Then the Holy Spirit can continue to weave our light bearing with all the other activities and circumstances that he has already orchestrated to convict our friends. This is Spirit-led evangelism. Evangelism should never be done alone. If we go about life and evangelism separately, our lives will be a refraction of

Christ, a distortion of Christianity. We are dependent beings, not independent, needing to continually live in and acknowledge the presence of Christ.

Light, Abiding, and Repentance

But light reveals not just the need of others, but our own deep need to see sin hidden in the dark places of our being. The type of abiding Scripture describes is an active and continual acknowledgment of being and living in the presence of God. If we abide in Christ we develop *a continual state of recognizing that we are in the presence of pure Holiness.* Abiding is not a simple non-responsive yielding to God, giving everything over to Him and going on auto-pilot so the Holy Spirit can take over. Abiding is not a blind or irresponsible attitude toward our own sinfulness. Rather, in order to come to understand the depth and breadth of God's love, we must come to grips with the depth and breadth of our personal sins. *In order to grow we must face and admit our own depravity.* This process is painful, fearful, and often lonely. When we stand naked in our sin before a God fully-clothed in pure holiness, shame and pain are standing there with us. But we will not be rejected, but can be cleansed through the blood of Christ. Therefore, we must confess our sins and not pretend to be something we are not. We need to repent of our wrong doing and should not be surprised as the Lord reveals even more of the ugliness of our sin. The Spirit of God is far more interested that we repent of the resentment we hold towards our spouse than our feeble exterior attempts of loving our spouse more. The Spirit wants us to repent of the jealousy and anger we harbor towards our boss rather than see our attempts to muster up a peaceful facial expression in the marketplace. You see, we have the ability to repent; we do not have the ability to produce the fruit of the Spirit by ourselves. Do what the Lord has commanded us to do, abide in Christ, and the love and peace desired for your spouse and boss will appear supernaturally. We must remember that in order to exhibit unconditional love we must be experiencing it from Christ (1 John 4:19; John 13:34-35).

When we honestly admit what we have done is wrong and take practical steps to avoid sin, God will use us in spite of our weakness and sin. *The deepest pain we ever experience grows out of getting a closer look at the ugliness of our own sin.* This process can be frightening and is always humbling, but it allows us to depend far more on God. The greatest atmosphere that the Lord has used to reveal the depth of my sin has been in living with my wife and four children. Oh, how my own selfishness and pride are exhibited as I live with my family. Have I been ashamed and humbled? Yes. Will I continue to be ashamed and humbled as God continues the process? Yes, if I want to develop intimacy with Him. But I have not been rejected by God; I am accepted and loved! Even in the midst of discovering my own sinfulness there is peace and acceptance in Christ. As my willingness to deal with my own sin grows, my dependence on Christ increases, my family relationships are deepened, and ministry opportunities grow.

First Love First

But even if my family relationships are not deepened or if ministry opportunities become nonexistent, I must still abide for that is the command and appeal of the Great Commandment: "Love the Lord your God with all your heart, soul, mind and strength" (Mark 12:30). The Great Commandment is primary; everything else, even though very important, is secondary. Our first love must be first.[9]

> I know your deeds and your toil and perseverance, and that you cannot endure evil men, and you put to the test those who call themselves apostles and they are not, and you found them to be false; and you have perseverance and have endured for My name's sake, and have not grown weary. But I have this against you, that you have left your first love. Remember therefore from where you have fallen, and repent and do the deeds you did at first; or else I am coming to you, and will remove your lampstand out of its place—unless you repent. (Revelation 2:2-5)

Here the Lord commends the church at Ephesus for its ministry influence. The Christians at Ephesus worked hard and persevered in spite of the trials and tests of evil people. God in many ways was pleased with their ministry activities, but they had missed God's primary concern: they had left their first love, the love for their Father in heaven. So God was not pleased with the church at Ephesus, and He is not pleased with us when we focus on the tasks of the Great Commission rather than on the process of intimacy with our Father. What do we need to do if we are caught in this failure? "Repent and return to our first love."

Conclusion

As we abide we come to see our own sin in a very different way. We come to understand and experience our sin as touching all of what we are. Our response must be to agree with God that that thought, that action, or that motive is sin. Agreeing and repenting are our responsibilities. God's commitment to us is to produce in us the fruit of His Spirit. We need not focus upon our personal growth; our growth is God's business. While physically maturing in my teenage years, it made no difference how much I wanted to grow. I did not grow any faster. But what I did do was eat, drink, and exercise. Did growth happen? Of course, but all my efforts and desires to be 180 pounds of solid muscle did not help. I took responsibility for what I was able to do and the growth process occurred.

Acknowledging our role, dealing with fears, and being honest about our pain are common in a healthy Christian journey. As my *dependence on Christ* increases so does the intensity of reflecting Christ. Reflecting Christ (manifesting the fruit of the Holy Spirit) will result in people being drawn closer to Christ or pushed further away. As we reflect God's light, people's sins are exposed. Those who are drawn by the Holy Spirit will be open to further interaction; those who are not drawn will retreat or attack. The results are not our concern or business. We do not convict, but we love and gently persuade, praying step-by-step for direction from the Holy Spirit. The pressure is off; we can enjoy the presence of God in our lives and minister in view of who we are in Christ.

Take advantage of your gifts, talents, and abilities and see them as a means of promoting His kingdom. God wastes neither time nor talent. He desires that you employ all He has given you to serve and proclaim him. *Remember, you are the most gifted, talented, and qualified person to do what God has called you to do.* Be content with the gifts, talents, and *limitations* the Lord has given you. Realizing that you have all you need to accomplish what the Lord has designed for you to do.

I often remind my martial arts students that our physical makeup is a factor in our flexibility. None of us had choices over our physical makeup which limits how high we can kick or if we can do a full split. So discover and accept your strengths and limitations, and train within those parameters.

Christians are all called to full-time ministry. The jobs, talents, and resources we possess have been given to us to facilitate our light bearing. Reflect Christ in your present situation and be content with what the Lord has called you to do. We have control over our talents and abilities; we do not have control over the choices and responses of others. Focus on Him and leave the "Godly results" up to God. Freedom really does result when we recognize that God has good works already ordained for us to accomplish (Ephesians 2:10). If God has already designed things for us to accomplish, He has or will equip us to do the work. So we do not need to compare ourselves to others and we can stop competing with them. The alternative is to compare ourselves and compete with others, but this will only result in arrogance, discouragement, lack of joy, and in not accomplishing the Lord's work.

Notes

[1] The Greek term translated "convict" here bears the sense and weight of "expose" and "convince", The Holy Spirit effects these actions in his ministry. His work is like a swordsman using a two-edged sword swinging it forward for the initial wounding or disabling blow while using the back stroke to cut deep for the fatal killing stroke: the Spirit first exposes and convinces us of our sinfulness before a righteous God and then presses on for complete conviction that, apart from Christ's righteousness and ability to save us from our sin, we are already condemned and on the way to judgment and destruction.

[2] Both Jesus and the Holy Spirit are even called our "advocate" (John 14:16, 26; 15:26; 16:7; and 1 John 1:1).

[3] Study the Gospel of John, Ephesians, and 1 John for a thorough treatment of the themes of light/darkness and love.

[4] Persuasion is the primary means Paul is seen using in the Book of Acts and Paul himself wrote that "knowing the fear of the Lord, we persuade men" concerning the truth of the gospel (2 Corinthians 5:22). John Stott has a superb discussion of the Christian's role and engagement with non-Christians in *Decisive Issues Facing Christians Today* (Grand Rapids: Fleming H. Revell, 1995), "Part One: Christians in a Non-Christian Society." D.A. Carson explores the same issues in more expanded form in *The Gagging of God* (Grand Rapids: Zondervan, 1996).

[5] The World Book Encyclopedia, Volume 12 – L (Chicago: World Book, Inc., 1984), p. 249.

[6] Ibid., p. 250.

[7] Ibid., pp. 250-250b.

[8] Ibid., p. 250b

CHAPTER 9

Continued Construction

I am writing to you, little children, because your sins are forgiven you
for His name's sake. I am writing to you, fathers,
because you know Him who has been from the beginning.
I am writing to you, young men,
because you have overcome the evil one.
I have written to you, children,
because you know the Father.
I have written to you, fathers,
because you know Him who has been from the beginning.
I have written to you, young men,
because you are strong and the word of God abides in you,
and you have overcome the evil one.
— 1 John 2:12-14 —

Imagine that your best friend, whom you have not seen for years, is visiting you. You are excited to see him and want to fill him in on what has been happening in your life since you last met. As soon as you pick him up at the airport, you begin to talk telling and asking all kinds of things while enjoying both the answers and the interaction. As you drive back to your home, you are pointing out where you work, the church you attend, and your favorite coffee shop. You do not feel compelled to tell him all these things; rather they naturally flow due to your deep friendship. This interactive process is similar to "taking every thought captive" (2 Corinthians 10:5). Unfortunately, few of us interact with Christ at this level. Just as a friendship grows between you and your best friend, so our relationship with Christ grows. Taking every thought captive must not be something we are compelled to do but something which comes *naturally*. This is a process done by God from within us rather than something we attempt to do in and of ourselves.

The following charts and discussion examine some of the characteristics of growth and relate them to our maturing relationship with Christ. According to 1 John

2:12-14, every Christian knows Christ in an experiential sense. The difference is the degree of knowing. The sequence of charts are given to help identify some of the characteristics that are commensurate to the degrees of knowing Christ.

Childhood – Imitating Others

Be imitators of me,
just as I also am of Christ.
— 1 Corinthians 11:1 —

As we saw earlier, the apostle Paul's great desire was to know Christ (Philippians 3:7-10). This is a knowing through experience, not mere knowledge about Christ. Experiential knowing consists of both a beginning and a process. The childhood stage is the beginning. It is initiated when an individual becomes a Christian, authentically committing his life to Christ.

Years ago while sitting with my wife and three children at the supper table, I leaned back and stretched. As my muscles loosened, I noticed that my then three-year-old daughter Christy was stretching her arms out and leaning back. If you had asked her, "What are you doing?," at three-years-old she could not have answered you. But if she could have, she might have said, "I don't have any idea what my dad is doing, but I want to be like him and so whatever he does I do." Children are tremendous imitators. They are constantly imitating and mimicking others. This is true also of new and young children in the faith as they look for godly individuals to *imitate.*

In my early years as a Christian I had the distinct privilege of being trained by two marvelous mentors, Ben Blackiston and Bob Lewis. Ben really helped to establish

me in my journey with the Lord while Bob helped me to think as a Christian. Ben was the Navigator staff representative at Penn State University in the early 1970s. I did not know much about the Christian faith, but whatever Ben did I soon followed in it too. Ben was my mentor. He had a relationship with Christ that I deeply desired. I did not know how to get that kind of relationship, so I figured if I hung around Ben long enough it would rub off on me. By the grace of God it did and I am to this day eternally thankful to God in using Ben in my life. I was a child hungering for intimacy with

Christ and the Lord used Ben as one of my mentors. Paul said, "Be imitators of me, just as I also am of Christ" (1 Corinthians 11:1). Paul recognized the importance of modeling, and he instructed others to imitate him. This is not inviting others to imitate perfect examples. It is encouraging others to *imitate those who are in the process and practice of knowing Christ*. When they stumble we are not to imitate their sin, we are to imitate their repentance.

Often an individual can be identified as a child in the faith when he responds to questions by quoting his mentor. Yet not every Christian has the privilege in the early years of his or her Christian faith of having an individual mentor. More often these Christians quote their pastor, favorite television or radio preachers, or Christian authors. Responses to questions like "What do you think of the end times?" are prefaced with "Well, Pastor Ben says... ," or "Chuck Swindoll points out that. . . ," or even "However, my seminary professor said. . . ." As you can see, the child is not yet equipped to say what he or she thinks due to a lack of *personal* familiarity with Scripture. He or she is much more secure with pointing to respected people who know God's word. This practice is another dimension of imitation and it should not be avoided or looked down upon. The child in Christ is simply imitating the mentor because he or she does not have a clue where to go to find out what the Bible says.

Similarly many times a child in the faith evaluates his or her relationship with Christ in light of how well he or she maintains the spiritual disciplines: quiet time, Scripture memory, Bible study, mediation, witnessing, etc. *The child believes that keeping the spiritual disciplines and his or her Christian life are synonymous.* The disciplines of the faith have become *ends* in and of themselves. This view, left uncorrected, results in tremendous guilt and anxiety when circumstances occur which do not permit the individual to practice the disciplines with any regularity. This is a common and immature view of the spiritual disciplines and their use and place in the Christian life.

Danger also lurks when individuals stagnate in the childhood stage and do not move on to becoming young adults in the faith. They go through life quoting the messages of others having no depth from their own Bible study, and they continue measuring their spiritual growth on the basis of their adherences to particular Christian activities. Scripture authenticates the legitimacy of babes in Christ, but children must grow up and grow deeper in their intimacy with Christ. How does this growth occur? What is it that feeds, nourishes, and strengthens us? It is by our feeding upon the word of God, taking it in, digesting it, and assimilating it into our whole-being. Without the experience of a personal encounter with the word of God, the growth process is greatly hindered.

Young Adult – Implanting God's Word/Learning to Obey

How can a young man keep his way pure?
By keeping it according to Thy word.
Thy word I have treasured in my heart,
that I may not sin against Thee.
— Psalm 119:9 & 11 —

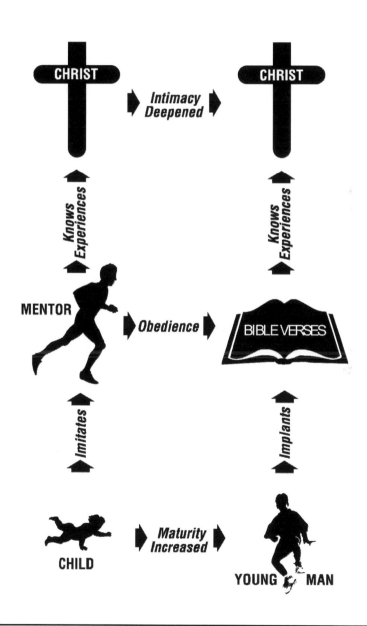

A valuable example that Ben modeled for me was the importance of God's word in his life. He did not do it by making or requiring me to adhere to a set of rules, rather he set the pace by his example. On many occasions I would have difficulty at work or have a conflict with Darlene, and I would call Ben on the phone. His response was predictable. He would listen intently and then invite me over to his house. When I arrived, he would greet me at the door with a smile and love that just beamed from his life. He usually offered me a cup of tea or hot coffee. Nancy, his wife, usually had some great pastries around, so I was adequately primed for any advice Ben had to offer. Ben would reach for his Bible and turn to relevant passages that spoke directly to my problems.

I remember one time in particular when he showed me that being the leader of my household did not mean me ordering and demanding things of my wife with no desire to hear her perspective. I was enlightened! Most of the time when Ben and I interacted over Scripture the focus was on *my* walk with God, not on my wife's or someone else's. Ben wisely realized that as my intimacy with Christ grew, my perspective of how I viewed my wife's problems and my own would change. The key was Ben's use of the *passages and verses* of Scripture to help me to come to experience Christ in a deeper way. As I continued to grow and as I was around Ben, my desire to obey the word of God rapidly accelerated. Not only was Ben's life a means to knowing Christ for me, so were the verses and passages of Scripture. Ben continued to be a model of going to God's word and of obeying it and I began to imitate his example and desired to *implant* the word of God into my heart so I could obey God.

I also remember the moment when the Spirit of God brought to my attention what he wanted me to do in regard to Ben's example of going to Scripture. I had a problem one morning and as usual I picked up the phone to call Ben. As I lifted the receiver, the question came into my mind, "What is Ben going to do?" The answer came streaking like a laser beam: he's going to pick up his Bible and see what God says about my problem. I suddenly realized that I could do that. Through the patient example of Ben, the Spirit showed me that I not only could go to His word for the answers to all of my problems, but that I had the responsibility to obey them as well.

Just as the primary verb of the lifestyle of a child in Christ is imitating, the verb for the young adult is *implanting*. The young adult desires to fill his or her life with the truths of Scripture which the Holy Spirit will bring to mind throughout life.

The young adult in the faith usually knows a lot about the Bible and frequently quotes verses related to diverse aspects of life. This can be very profitable as long as this person realizes that implanting the word of God into his or her heart is not the ultimate purpose of Scripture; the purpose of *implanting the word of God into one's heart is to foster intimacy with and obedience to Christ.* The purpose of Bible knowledge is not to be able to impress fellow Christians or to think that knowing something in the mind is sufficient for growth. A wise mentor will regularly help a new or young disciple to realize the value of obeying the word of God. Even obedience itself is not the end of knowing Scripture, but rather intimacy with Christ is. True obedience grows out of a close walk with Christ.

Unlike the child, who often views keeping the spiritual disciplines as ends in themselves, the young adult comes to view the disciplines as *means* to an end. In other words, these external activities serve as vehicles to develop intimacy with Christ. A common danger of this view is that too often people are looking to the disciplines as a way to Christ, and when they do not feel that their intimacy with Christ is growing, they usually increase, intensify, or multiply these external activities. Stagnation, guilt, and a disenchanted perspective of the disciplines often arise when one becomes stuck in this phase of growth instead of moving onto the maturity of adulthood in the faith.

Adulthood – Internalized Biblical Principles/Abiding in Christ
You shall love the LORD your God with all your heart,
and with all your soul, and with all your mind
— Matthew 22:37; Jesus citing Deuteronomy 6:5 —

As the young adult continues to grow in obedience to the verses of Scripture, *trust* in Christ deepens and knowledge of and intimacy with Christ further develop. The young adult is growing into a mature adult in the faith. People to imitate are not looked for, nor are verses of Scripture needed for every decision in life. Rather, *biblical principles* are focused upon, as contained and revealed in the verses and passages of Scripture. A principle is a fundamental law or truth which can provide the basis for additional truth as well as give direction for the development of ministry.

We have seen that the Christian's primary principle of life is the Great Commandment: love the Lord with all of who and what we are and have. By loving God totally, I am prepared to love my neighbor as myself (Matthew 22:39). I have found that as my intimacy with Christ deepens, I am confronted with my personal depravity at a deeper level. As I repent and depend upon Christ even more, I am freed to a greater degree to love my neighbor as myself. Like Isaiah, I have come to see myself in a clearer manner and am enabled to see others in a truer perspective as well. As I grow in intimacy with Christ, even the love I have for myself is altered. My self-love (narcissism) is slowly transformed into a God love (agape) of myself. As I continue to see myself *in Christ,* as God sees me, I love (agape) myself differently. Because of my personal experience of God's agape I am now enabled by the Holy Spirit to manifest agape, a fruit of the Spirit, towards others. Hence, the second great commandment is a fruit of the first great commandment.

As I grow in peace with my Father in heaven, I grow in peace with myself. I learn that the door and every window of my house are uniquely crafted by the loving hands of God. I realize that I had no choice in the matter and that I have been equipped to accomplish what the Lord has already set in place for me. As peace with God and peace with myself grow, I encounter a peace with others unlike anything I have experienced. I no longer need to compete with non-Christians and Christians to feel good about myself. Rather, I have a sane estimate (humility) of who I am and my self-worth is found and grounded in God. I am growing in freedom to respond to others in view of who Christ is in and through me.

The adult Christian has walked with God for years and desires to serve Him out of love and gratitude (Hebrews 12:28), not because a mentor serves God nor because a verse of Scripture indicates service is a good idea. These two reasons are not wrong, rather the adult has just come to know Christ at such depth that his focus is loving God out of gratitude. Our journey with the Lord is a process, and for many of us we may be an adult in one area of our lives, a young adult in another dimension, and even childish in another. Regardless, we must continue to abide in him.

The adult practices the presence of God regularly and naturally. The Spirit has probably used many mentors and verses to move the adult in this direction, but now others and verses are not the motivators. Instead, past years of experiencing Christ have so impacted the adult that he or she has *internalized* the principles of Scripture. So, we can naturally agree with St. Augustine's perspective, "Love God and do whatever you want" (a paraphrase). The primary focus is Christ, and there is a natural and constant dialogue with Him.

The adult has grown greatly in experiencing the biblical truth "Cease striving and know that I am God" (Psalm 46:10) and has learned that God wants us to abandon our self-will. The Lord often does this by getting us into Isaiah's situation where the only reasonable response is, "Woe is me!" and we have stopped striving after what

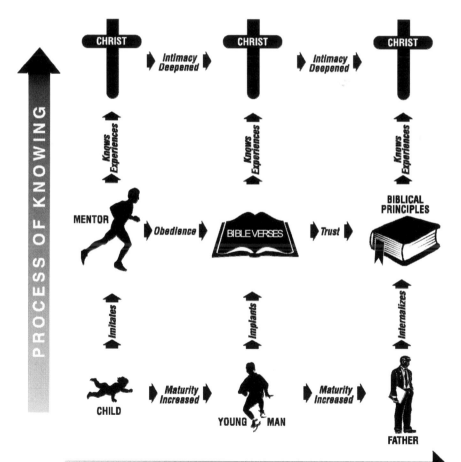

the world says is necessary in order to feel secure and worthwhile. More and more as we follow the Shepherd we experience the truth of "I shall not want" (Psalm 23:1). When we have intimacy with Christ, there is nothing lacking in our lives – we have what we truly need. *But if we continue to strive for the things of the world or even to accomplish great things for God, we will miss God Himself.* Cease striving and know (experience) that He is God. Do not be like Martha, concerned about all the things of life. Martha needed to learn the lesson her sister Mary had already learned; that there is really only one thing in life worth doing – loving God (Luke 10:38-42). Apart from Christ we are inadequate, we are failures. We were designed and created to live in Christ. Striving is effort expended for ourselves even though the things we strive for may be viewed as spiritual. As we grow in this truth (living in Christ) experientially, we will cease to strive after the world and even the spiritual activities as ends or means, and realize that *we do not need a way to The Way.* The Way lives in us; therefore, experience His presence as Mary did and stop the striving like Martha.

Comparing the Child, Young Adult, and Adult Christian

Let's select the spiritual discipline of what is commonly called a "quiet time" (QT) to further clarify the differences between these three growing individuals. By QT I mean a daily devotional, usually done in the morning, where a specified time is spent in reading Scripture and in prayer. If asked why he or she has a QT, the child in the faith might point to a mentor and say how his or her example has encouraged the practice of having a regular QT. If you ask the same question of the young adult, he or she may respond by quoting a verse like Mark 1:35, "And in the early morning, while it was still dark, He [Jesus] arose and went out and departed to a lonely place, and was praying there" and may reasonably reply, "You see, as I studied the Scriptures, I discovered that Jesus had a QT and, therefore, so do I." But if you ask the adult about his QT the response might be, "I have a QT throughout my entire day. I have found that fifteen to thirty minutes in the morning just isn't enough time with my heavenly Father. So I have come to spend my entire day interacting with Him about problems, relationships, joys, and sorrows. I find myself constantly taking my thoughts captive to Him and conversing with Him. I not only need to do this, but I greatly desire this continual communion."

A Way to The Way?

Wesley Nelson writes:

Because prayer is revitalized through fellowship with Christ, there is a tendency to look upon prayer as a way to Christ, and to try vainly to pray more fervently in order to come closer to Him. The Bible witnesses to Christ, and when Christ is near, the Bible is a new book. Therefore, some torment themselves for not reading or studying it more faithfully in order to know Him better. Christ is the Way to the Bible, as He is to prayer. The Spirit of Christ Himself must speak through the pages of the Scriptures before they can become meaningful. The time of daily personal devotions becomes a more blessed experience to those who know Christ intimately. Sometimes this tends to be looked upon as a way to Christ, and the responsibility to keep it only adds to the burden of a troubled conscience. The sheep do not come to the still waters to find the Shepherd. It is the Shepherd Himself who leads them beside the still waters. Christ is immediately available right where we are, as we are. He in turn becomes the way to these various means of worship. He leads us into those forms of personal devotion and worship which are most adapted to each one's spiritual needs.[1]

The essential point here is that the spiritual disciplines are not ways to the Way. Jesus *is* The Way. He is able to direct us into many diverse forms of worship and pleasure of the Lord. As I grow in enjoying the presence of the Lord in the everyday affairs of my life, I have found that the Lord leads me freely and often with much variety to experience different forms of worship. I no longer view my relationship with Christ as doing an activity or striving to perform particular rituals with the anticipation of coming close to God. Rather, I look towards Him at any moment and interact with Him and enjoy His presence continually. When I turn away from Him and sin, I (can) quickly turn back to Him, acknowledge my sin, and repent of the thought or act. My communion with Christ continues and neither of us is surprised at my sin.

The beauty of this lifestyle is that this Christian, lost in Christ, is not even aware of the virtues beaming from his or her life: *Christ has become the center and focus for this person's entire existence.* This mature adult has stopped striving and has learned to rest in the Lord in all circumstances and all things. Now we can better understand why a person like Eric Little who was designed to run fast could say, "When I run, I feel His pleasure."[2]

Perhaps you have not been created to run fast, but you have been created with many talents, abilities, and gifts that uniquely qualify you to do the very things God designed for you. But remember, Eric's primary purpose was not to run but to practice the presence of God in all that he did. Do not create a division between the physical and the spiritual. You are created a spiritual being; glorify God whether you eat, drink, or run (1 Corinthians 10:31). As you do any of these things, you will experience the abundant life in Christ.

Conclusion

The word of God and prayer are certainly used by the Spirit of God in our lives. We must make sure that Scripture and prayer do not become idols or alternatives to the primary process of abiding with Christ. Roy Hession says it well:

Under the law with its ten-fold lash,

Learning, alas, how true,

That the more I tried the sooner I died,

While the law cried, You! You!! You!!!

Hopelessly still did the battle rage,

"O wretched man" my cry,

And deliverance I sought by solemn penance bought,

While my soul cried I! I!! I!!!

Then came a day when my struggling ceased,

And trembling in every limb,

At the foot of the Tree where One died for me,

I sobbed out, HIM! HIM!! HIM!!![3]

Even in this poem we see the development in thinking and of life experience. All three stages, child, young adult, and adult, are necessary but the ultimate purpose of life regardless of the stage is to know HIM.

Notes

[1] Quote from Wesley Nelson found in Roy Hession, *We Would See Jesus,* p. 67.

[2] *Chariots of Fire* (Burbank, CA: Warner Communications Co.).

[3] Hession, p. 61.

CHAPTER 10

Helping Others Rebuild

I planted, Apollos watered, but God was causing the growth.
So then neither the one who plants nor the one who waters is anything,
but God who causes the growth. Now he who plants and he who waters
are one; but each will receive his own reward according to his own labor.
— 1 Corinthians 3:6-8 —

The planting and watering processes in our lives are our responsibilities; causing people to grow is God's responsibility. We cannot make people grow and we should not try to make them grow. Even though planting and watering are our responsibilities, the Lord empowers us as well. Planting God's word in relevant ways through meaningful relationships will often be watered by someone else days and even years later. Planting can be understood as sharing the word of God so it is heard and understood by another. Watering is relating and interacting with someone in such a manner that the previously planted seeds of God's word are understood in a deeper sense leading to the fruit of righteous living. The Lord uses the plows of pain and suffering to turn up the rocks and weeds in our lives that are hindering our relationships with Him. The Lord's plowing process often opens people up to the seeds that we plant.

"Now the God of peace ... equip you in every good thing to do His will, working in us that which is pleasing in His sight, through Jesus Christ, to whom be the glory forever and ever. Amen" (Hebrews 13:21). God energizes us; we do not do it ourselves. We need to keep this in mind as we develop relationships and train others. God will cause them to grow from the inside out; He will bring it to pass. We must learn to discern what the Lord is doing in an individual's life.

On Being a Stumbling Block

Jesus gave His disciples a stern warning:

> And He said to His disciples, "It is inevitable that stumbling blocks should come, but woe to him through whom they come! It would be better for

him if a millstone were hung around his neck and he were thrown into the sea, than that he should cause one of these little ones to stumble." (Luke 17:1-2)

"Little ones" refers not to physical children but to new or young believers in the faith. The point of concern is that we do not require activities and programs which from a superficial standpoint look okay but in reality are a detriment to someone coming to Christ or growing in Him. Becoming a stumbling block to someone's intimacy with Christ occurs quite frequently by well-intentioned Christians sincerely attempting to help someone grow in Christ. Even Christian leaders train people with little or no regard for their unique qualities and characteristics. Our focus must not be on strategy or the newest packaged approach to discipleship but on Christ. Anything that gets in the way of Christ must be eliminated. Peter once was severely reprimanded by Christ: "Get behind Me Satan; for you are not setting your mind on God's interests, but man's" (Mark 8:33). In principle He was saying, "Peter, you have something other than God's will in mind – this is evil, satanic. Get out of the way; focus on Christ!" We make the mistake of focusing upon our plan, our task, and our ideas rather than upon Christ. We must not see Jesus as a means to our ends or substitute anything else for Him. The focus is upon relationship, not ritual. We must avoid the error of the Scribes and Pharisees who elevated their ideas and traditions above the things of God.

As we understand what planting and watering mean, the possibilities for being stumbling blocks decrease. Be careful not to turn the strategies that helped you to grow into principles for everyone else. Just as the Lord exercises great variety in making all the flowers of the world, permit Him the same freedom to help His disciples to grow differently than you. For a moment, imagine you are well-known for your beautiful rose garden. People in your community know you for the size and beauty of the many varieties of roses in your front yard. One day a friend asks you to help him grow a daisy garden. So you set about to grow daisies the same as you grow roses. Since both roses and daisies are flowers you know they need sunshine, water, and nutrients. You decide that since your roses look great, so will your neighbor's daisies. But the daisies just do not grow very well. What is the problem? The problem is that you cannot grow daisies by treating them like roses. Why did God make daisies? He did it because He is a God of variety, and He did not want every flower to look like a rose.

Each of us requires food, clothing, and shelter just as flowers need nutrients, sunshine, and water. However, the amount of food and sunshine required for a rose is different from that of a daisy, and so it is also with Christ's disciples. Therefore, remember, God does not make every person alike nor do we grow in our walk with Him the same way.

Even though the individuals we are attempting to help have the same five windows and a door to their life just like we do, the relationships and dimensions of each is different by the design of God. To know and truly appreciate people is a challenge. F.B. Huey Jr., a close friend of mine and a godly man who teaches Old Testament in Forth Worth, Texas, once said, "I learn things about God by getting to know other people."[1] Each of us in a very real way can reflect glimmers of God through the unique combinations of our temperaments, abilities, and virtues just as a painting gives us an idea of what the artist is like.

Truth and Relationships: A Necessary Synthesis

Ultimately, we want to be imitators of Christ and we want to help others to do the same. A very important ingredient in this process is helping to bring truth and relationships together. Paul describes a beautiful synthesis of the two where he says, "Having thus a fond affection for you, we were well-pleased to impart to you not only the gospel of God but also our own lives, because you had become very dear to us" (1 Thessalonians 2:8). But many Christians embrace one at the expense of the other.

There are those who study the word of God so intensely that they do not have time for people. Truth to many of these pastors and scholars becomes the focus, and many arrogantly treat the truth of God as personal property. They have overlooked, ignored, or never learned the truth that knowledge breeds arrogance and love edifies (1 Corinthians 8:1). These Christians have come to view truth, particularly the Bible, as information with the sole purpose of introducing or designing a whole new worldview. There is no doubt that the Bible speaks of reality in quite different terms compared to the views of our humanistic societies. But the Bible is more than just information about reality and it calls us to far more than just knowledge about its content.

At the other extreme there are those well-meaning Christians who focus on relationships at the expense of truth. These are individuals who have many relationships, but because they know very little of the truth they live at odds with God's word. They even compromise biblical teaching in morality for the sake of maintaining or developing their relationships with others.

So on the one hand we have knowledge that by itself breeds arrogance and on the other we have relationships without boundaries or restrictions. Truth is given by God to us to provide limits and boundaries in relationships while relationships are given to provide the arena in which we live out the truth. Truth without relationship breeds the sin of arrogance while the aftermath of relationships without truth are sinful relationships. Truth and relationships are part of God's design for our lives, but are meant to exist *together*.

John V. Tailor shared a very sad story in a 1971 lecture at the School of World Mission of Fuller Theological Seminary:

> When my son decided to give up on the Church, he said to me, "Father, that man [the preacher] is saying all of the right things, but he isn't saying them to anybody. He doesn't know where I am and it would never occur to him to ask!"[2]

Most often people need to live and share the information of Scripture in relevant ways to stimulate people to faith in Christ: "And let us *consider* how to stimulate one another to love and do good deeds" (Hebrews 10:24).[3] This relevant stimulating requires that we become students of people not only in observation but in inquiry. If we do not take the time to ponder, to think about those we are speaking to, the chances are we will not be an encouragement to them. I find these principles very helpful when interacting with my wife and four children. They are different from me. When I respond to them without considering who they are, our conversations and relationships generally do not go too well.

Truth, the Bible, and Disciplemaking

Jesus' communicative style was uniquely woven around the people to whom He ministered. Paul also used a similar strategy: "To the Jew I became a Jew, to those under the Law I came under the Law, to those without the Law I acted without the Law, to the weak, I was weak, that I may save some" (1 Corinthians 9:19-23).

In the discipling process, the core and ultimate grid for all truth is the written word of God, biblical truth, the absolute standard. The Bible serves as our final authority and it helps us to discover true reality in order to discern the real from the unreal. The propositional truth of Scripture is found at the heart of whole-person discipleship. However, as Arthur F. Holmes so aptly states, "All truth is God's truth" – God is the ultimate source of *all truth,* whether it is in the Bible or not.[4] Jesus said, "I am the way, and the truth, and the life" (John 14:6). He was not simply indicating that He knows truth; rather He was saying "I am the embodiment of all truth." We as

Christians do not need to be fearful of truth regardless of its source, even if the truth is revealed in natural revelation identified through the vehicle of the social or natural sciences. The Bible serves as the ultimate interpretive grid for all 'truth'. "Experiential Truth" is to be understood as truth lived out, whether the truth has its source in Scripture (special revelation, which must be primary) or creation (natural revelation).

To Program or Not to Program? – That Is the Question

Whole-person discipleship is not a mechanical process involving contrived programs. We must avoid the type of Christianity described by Eddie Gibbs wherein "religious groups develop from men to movements, turn into machines and eventually become monuments.[5] Similarly, T. F. O'Dea observes that "To embody the sacred in a vehicle is to run the risk of its secularization."[6] Remembering that we are all handmade by the fingers of God we need to disciple people in the light of who they are rather than approaching them as if they were identical cars on an auto assembly line.

I have thought a great deal about why we have a tendency to want to deal the same way with everyone. Immanuel Kant has helped me here with his distinction between that which I cannot see (the noumenal) and that which I can see (the phenomenal). The phenomenal is that which can be empirically observed. This is what science looks at in its quest for truth. The noumenal cannot be seen and observed and thus is often neglected by the hard sciences. Regardless, since God has given us creation and His Word, we can be better stewards of His command to have dominion over the earth through the use of science as we empirically investigate the 'phenomenal' world. Through theology we discern the truth of Scripture and thus develop our biblical grid that sifts all the data of science.

Now my fear is that since our society has become so interested and concerned with what can be seen that we have forgotten that which we cannot see. This may be observed in the emphasis on measuring a person's growth in Christ in ways that can be observed outwardly. I am not opposed to this as long as we do not forget the unseen. But this is exactly what I think has happened. The discipleship programs I am aware of taking place in the churches today emphasize activities as an end in themselves. When asked why this is so, the response is, "Well, we can measure how many verses someone memorizes, and how many daily quiet times someone has." But biblical discipleship is not a program, it is a lifestyle. What about the unseen? What about that dimension of humanity which cannot be seen (abiding with Christ), but does produce in our lives the fruit of the Spirit? Should not this area be a concern for whole-person discipleship? The fruit of the Spirit (Galatians 5:22-23) may not be measured in the same way we count quiet times, but the manifestation of the fruit of the Spirit is the means by which we can measure our spiritual growth and maturity. Love, joy, peace, etc., are all empirically discernible and measurable. Jesus measured love when He said, *"Greater love has no one than this, that one lay down his life for his friends"* (John 15:13), and Paul measured humility, obedience, and sacrifice when he wrote "He humbled Himself by becoming obedient *to the point of death, even death on a cross"* (Philippians 2:8). We could find other examples for love and each of the other fruit of the Spirit, but these should be sufficient to underscore that they are the true indicators of intimacy with Christ and are seen in a disciple as he abides in Christ. When we focus upon the disciplines, the fruit of the Spirit are not automatically guaranteed. The disciplines can be molded and shaped in light of culture and personality to facilitate an atmosphere for the fruit of the Spirit to be manifested.

Often in Christian development there is an attempt to push the unseen into the realm of the seen – this is dangerous. Whole-person discipleship is a whole-life approach to the development of humanity and must include both that which is seen and that which cannot be seen. Perhaps with our overemphasis on what we can see we have lost the very heart of discipleship – a relationship with Christ. I have trained many people to excel in the observable disciplines and yet many did not grow in Him. Dietrich Bonhoeffer understood this:

When the Bible speaks of following Jesus, it is proclaiming a discipleship which will liberate mankind from all man-made dogmas, from every burden and oppression, from every anxiety and torture which afflicts the conscience. If they follow Jesus, men escape from the hard yoke of their own laws, and submit to the kindly yoke of Jesus Christ. But does this mean that we ignore the seriousness of His commands? Far from it. We can only achieve perfect liberty and enjoy fellowship with Jesus when His command, His call to absolute discipleship, is appreciated in its entirety.[7]

Along the same lines, Derek Tidball says:

The ethics of Christian discipleship then was not a rigid and inflexible set of dogmatic responses which could be automatically put into operation by any Christian anywhere as soon as he had time to consult the rule book. They were much more a living application of various Christian doctrines and principles as the occasion demanded. Sometimes the situation demanded an emphasis on the conversionist approach and sometimes the emphasis was on a revolutionist approach or on one of the other responses to the world. But always they were a clear application of the apostolic teaching and divinely revealed principles.[8]

There are many approaches to discipleship that produce a mindless and shallow faith. Christian leaders need to be particularly careful not to manipulate international congregations into becoming *American* or *European* churches. This approach is not only self-centered, but a degradation of humanity and culture. Missiologist Paul Hiebert persuasively argues this:

> In particular, we from the West must guard against a mechanistic reductionism. We tend to think in terms of cause and effect and believe that we can solve our problems and achieve our goals if only we have the right methods or answers. This approach has made us masters over much of nature, but it has also led us to see other people as objects that we can manipulate if we use the right formulas. In fact, even the social sciences can be seen as new "formulas" if they are misused. The gospel calls us to see people as human beings, and any effective mission action begins by building relationships not programs.
>
> A mechanistic approach also tempts us to seek to control God for our own purposes. We set the agenda and try to make God do our bidding. But Scripture always calls us away from this type of magic and toward worship and obedience. The missionary task is first the work of God, and we must follow his lead. This does not eliminate the need to plan or strategize. But it does mean that we must do so with an attitude of submission to God and a recognition that he acts when he chooses, often in ways that we cannot understand.[9]

Hiebert concludes his argument for holism by saying that we must learn the truth from theology and the sciences, and weave these truths into a comprehensive understanding of people as whole- beings, with the humble awareness that our knowledge is incomplete.[10]

Personalized Environmental Control

It is not the discipler's job to make individuals do anything. Instead, prayerfully help them to *discover* their strengths and limitations, *facilitate* an environment for development and liberation through the ministry of the Holy Spirit. We plant and water, but it is God who causes the growth (1 Corinthians 3:6). God is the active agent in the discipling process; disciplers are *facilitators* who need to know their limits and responsibilities before God. This means that we should not attempt to superimpose our pet programs or methods on others, but rather to pray for discernment and look through the windows of their lives for what the Holy Spirit is doing, and then to facilitate God's growth process. Recently, Shannon, my youngest daughter entered our family room very angry about a book she was required to read for school. She said, "Dad, I really don't like the way this author talks about God!" The author didn't properly attribute honor and reverence to the Lord. I responded, "Shannon, you are experiencing righteous anger." I then proceeded to explain my comment in more detail. I facilitated Shannon's growth by explaining that her concern was prompted by the Holy Spirit moving in her life. A disciplemaker can establish either an environment that encourages growth or one that represses or hinders growth. We must be very cautious about hindering the growth of God's kingdom, for it is His kingdom we are building, not our own (Matthew 18:6 and 6:33).

We must also remember that the Holy Spirit is in many ways unpredictable. What the Holy Spirit does via the climate you attempt to create may not be what you expect or even want. Yet, here is where the knowledge of our role and God's role is necessary: we plant and water, but God causes the growth.

Jesus ministered by keying in on what others were occupied with in life. Here are a few examples of what people were concerned with: The woman at the well – water; the rich young ruler – how to have eternal life; the woman caught in adultery – forgiveness.

I really do not know how God causes people to grow. I can relate a lot to the sower Jesus talked about who casts seed in the proper environment (soil), but when the plant came up, he had no idea of how it grew (Mark 4:26-29).

It is important to realize that whole-person discipleship is not encouraged by the adherence to rules and obligations. As my friend Jim Terry once said, "It's not necessarily adding things on, but helping people throw their limitations off."[11] Freedom results when we discover that obedience does not mean that we must know what to do all of the time: sometimes we just do not know what the right decision is, but a decision needs to be, must be, made. Rather, freedom and obedience is *serving* God out of gratitude.

Sometimes I am not sure whether I should let my children participate in certain activities. The Bible does not tell me if I should allow them to go to a particular party or event, but as I look to my Heavenly Father and commune with Him and ask for wisdom, I make a decision, *trusting* Him. This is a practical application of the greatest commandment, "AND YOU SHALL LOVE THE LORD YOUR GOD WITH ALL YOUR HEART, AND WITH ALL YOUR SOUL, AND WITH ALL YOUR MIND, AND WITH ALL YOUR STRENGTH" (Mark 12:30). The relationship between the two greatest commandments is vital; for as we love and experience God, we discover a proper view of our self and of others.

Thus, we become better equipped to fulfill the second greatest commandment, "YOU SHALL LOVE YOUR NEIGHBOR AS YOURSELF" (Mark 12:31). This love is not a selfish love but action that cares for oneself. This action, which expresses love of self, occurs within each of the six dimensions of our humanity: rational, physical, moral, volitional, emotional, and relational. If we are to love others as ourselves, this love must be whole-person in nature, considering all six dimensions of our humanity.

Robert Coleman once said to me the following:

> It must be remembered that our emphasis must not only be on the practical, but there must also exist a strong focus on the holiness of God. If you only emphasize the practical without the holiness of God, one becomes complacent.[12]

To emphasize the holiness of God without the practical implications is disobedience. This balance must be a living reality in whole-person discipleship. Through the holiness of God liberation takes place, not by our plans and programs. We are to be the light of the world (Matthew 5:16). Whole-person discipleship embraces the need to cast light which can be seen through the windows and doors of our lives. We must recall that God is truth and God is light, and that as we practice the truth we walk in the light (John 3:21). This light reveals to us further our need *for* Christ and for service *with* Christ.

How I Discern God Working in My Life

The following is a personal taxonomy of how the Spirit of God tends to work in my life. I do not believe He operates in everyone's life the same way. However, reflecting on this information has helped me to better understand a process of how the Lord tends to work in my own life. Attempting to apply this to your life will probably serve little purpose, yet I suggest that you take the time to identify potential relationships among the following aspects, as well as others, in your own life.

A major short coming of this taxonomy is that it tends to characterize life in a straight, linear manner: A+B=C. Approaching life in this fashion tends to focus on events rather than on process – *avoid this error.* God can meet us any place and at any time; He is not limited. In reality, the following areas probably all work together and interact in ways that I simply do not, maybe cannot, understand. Yet, the relationship of these concepts has served in helping me to identify, in a limited way, the sanctification process in my own life. Here we go.

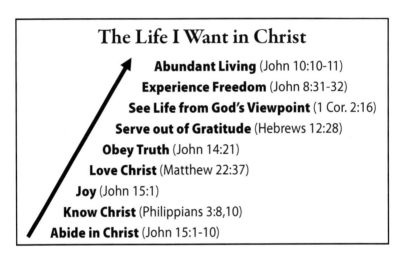

As I *abide* in the presence of God, I have come to *know* Him more intimately. *Joy* has been the refreshing fruit of our union and I desire to *love* Him more deeply. As our love continues, my *obedience* grows as does my *service* out of gratitude. This process leads me to a new perspective of God, myself, others, and creation. *I am set free* from the bondage of sin and the abundant life Christ promises is experienced.

A Lifestyle of Being with Jesus

Because Jesus wanted to impart a lifestyle, He commanded people to *be with Him* (Mark 3:14). This *"with Him"* principle required more than just verbal proclamation. Jesus wanted people around Him to *follow Him, not to just listen to Him* (Luke 9:23). "To follow" someone in the biblical sense requires more of one's humanity than just listening to someone's teaching and agreeing with it. Christ calls people to a lifestyle instead of a program.

Combining example with proclamation is the best, and most balanced and biblically-based, model for expressing the Christian life. In the following chart, Dabner[13] shows the importance of combining persuasive proclamation with personal example.

Percent of Things We Remember

	After 3 Hours	After 3 Days
What We Hear	70%	10%
What We See	72%	20%
What We See & Hear	86%	65%

Dr. Ted Ward has said that "truth is not personal property."[14] This is particularly relevant to discipleship, because discipleship is the living out of truth that we proclaim not the accumulation of truth. Truth exhibited by both the Christian's life and lips will be used by the Holy Spirit to convict people of the lies that they manifest in the various dimensions of their own lives, and it provides a model for genuine freedom. We must never forget that the central objective of Jesus' incarnation is to set people *free* from sin and its power, and to reconcile them with God. We learn from the great apostle Paul that *there is no condemnation for those who are in Christ Jesus* (Romans 8:1-17). Christ sets us free! "It was for freedom that Christ set us free; therefore keep standing firm and do not be subject again to a yoke of slavery" (Galatians 5:1). We are no longer slaves of sin, but rather we are slaves of a living and loving God and of righteousness (Romans 6:15-23). Through this freedom and by abiding in Christ, we are able to relate properly to God, ourselves, others, and creation (Romans 12:11; 4:18; Colossians 3:24; Galatians 5:13). The beauty and paradox of this slavery is that we are freed to do that which we know and want to be and do. The life I want in Christ is a life of freedom. But freedom is more than doing. *The freedom Jesus offers is not the ability to do what I want to do, it is rather the enablement through abiding to be what God designed me to be.* The doing of righteousness follows; doing always follows from being (Luke 1:74-75; Romans 6:16-18,20).

A study of God's attributes is an amazing thing. Omniscience ("all knowing"), omnipotence ("all powerful"), and omnipresence ("present everywhere at all times") are among some of the more familiar attributes of God. But where in Scripture are we ever commanded to be omniscient, omnipotent, or omnipresent? But we are commanded "You shall be holy, for I am holy" (1 Peter 1:16 citing Leviticus 11:44ff).

Holiness is not an attribute of God but instead it is his very nature (set apart; moral perfection). Even in heaven Christians will not possess all of God's attributes but more importantly we will be holy (positionally and practically) just as He is – We will be like Him!

Thus, in our disciplemaking we need to keep the core value of God's nature(holiness) – in sight. When our strategies stray from this, we become stumbling blocks as disciplemakers.

Discipling & Freedom

The focus of whole-person discipleship is to help people discover this freedom and to encourage an atmosphere conducive for learning and living a liberated lifestyle in Christ. Just as captives released from an extended stay in the darkness of the dungeon need time to adjust to the light, so the discipler must be patient with the Christian he is discipling as he or she adjusts to the light (truth) of a new and radical lifestyle. Christ is not simply interested in adorning the windows or in interior decorating; He completely rebuilds our lives (2 Corinthians 5:17). This is major construction and involves a lot of failure on our part. *Complete obedience entails regular failure.* Failure requires patience from us all. Hiebert says, "Our task is not to stand in condemnation of young Christians, but to help them overcome the sins that so quickly beset us all."[15]

Thinking of our house illustration, we need to see the six dimensions as being connected by the hallways of the house and all having inherent importance and value. But bondage can develop when we overemphasize one dimension of our humanity over the others. For example, spending eight hours each day in body building (physical) or becoming so wrapped up in the lives of our children (relational) produces the result that the rest of the dimensions suffer. While there may be times of individual focus on certain dimensions, we should remember that they are all connected and need attention and care. Again we come back to *balance.*

Situational Teaching: Whatever Is There, Use It

Situational teaching is using whatever is at your experiential disposal in any teaching situation. We can use the five senses (hearing, sight, touch, taste, and smell) common to humanity to draw people to Christ through the use of storytelling and questions. Our five senses are the bullets that fill the twin guns of storytelling and questions. The task is not to shoot our audiences, but to skillfully fire our guns in such a way that the attention of the audience is not only caught but that their desire to learn is facilitated.

Jesus was able to take *anything* around Him and use it to teach. There are at least three reasons why He was able to do this. First, Jesus knew the Father. Second, He was very familiar with creation (nature, culture, geography, etc.). Third, He knew his audience: He was a student of people. Jesus utilized situational teaching throughout His ministry. Study the way He taught the rich man (Luke 18:18-23) and Mary and Martha (Luke 10:38-42).

Situational teaching involves more than a superficial understanding of these three ingredients. Situational teaching engages the use of questions and storytelling which are relevant to the person(s) spoken to and at the same time clarifies the truth(s). Simultaneously, we trust the Holy Spirit to enlighten the individual(s) we are addressing.

One word of caution needs to be given with reference to our intent. We are not in the discipling process alone; we never were and should never act as though the Spirit of God is not involved. *When our personal worth or self-esteem is evaluated on the basis of someone's growth or on statistics, we often attempt to assume the work of God by trying to make people grow. This is a dangerous situation in which to find yourself actively involved.*

Allow me to clarify three terms: coercion, manipulation, and persuasion. I can use coercion in my Jujutsu training by physically twisting an individual's wrist and *make* them do things that they may *not* want to do. At times police officers have to do this as part of their job description. We, however, are speaking of helping others grow in intimacy with Christ and we must respect their volitional dimension and not physically manhandle them. But of course, you already knew you should not use neck chokes when sharing the gospel.

But what about manipulation? Manipulation is placing people in situations where they must choose to do something that they do not want to do or to violate an idea, principle, or relationship that is valuable to them. They are placed into a situation to make a decision that is for your benefit and not theirs. Think of a father who has sincerely tried to share the gospel with his son, but to no apparent avail. He then says, "Son, if you really love me you will accept Jesus." This is manipulation.

There is a great cartoon satirically illustrating this point. It portrays a Christian of the Crusades on horseback pointing his spear at a Muslim asking the question, "Would you like to repent or suffer the consequences?" *We are not called to use coercion or manipulation; we are called to persuade people to the truth.* With respect to their physical, moral, volitional, emotional, relational, and rational abilities, we are to reason together with them recognizing the existence of spiritual warfare, their blinded state, and our role to plant and water the seed of God's Word while trusting the Holy Spirit to do His work. This approach to ministry honors God and frees us to minister out of obedience and trust, not obligation and guilt.

Usually, Christian leaders are very familiar with the truth of Scripture but too often become satisfied with informing other's minds rather than helping them learn to obey. Scripture and experience have shown that this approach most often leaves Christians with head-knowledge far beyond their life experience. Often the desired outcomes of our teaching do not occur because we do not understand one or more of the *three necessary ingredients* of situational teaching {knowing God, knowing creation, and knowing people} or because we have attempted to coerce or manipulate. Or maybe the Holy Spirit has something else in mind and we just are not in touch with Him. Relevant storytelling and questions open up numerous avenues to pursue in ministering and discipling as we look into the various windows of people's lives, and may also help them in becoming more intimate with Christ.

Situational Teaching: Bob, Tom, and I

A personal example might help synthesize all of what has been said in this chapter. A few years ago I was hired as a part-time racquetball instructor. The 70,000 square-foot facility was brand new and smelled like a new car and everything inside the building was still smooth to the touch. Before this fitness center opened, employees would stand in separate areas while groups of new members would move from station to station to hear the employee's three-minute presentation. My station was the brand new lightning-fast racquetball courts. While waiting for the group to come through, I sat with a young male co-worker who had just graduated from college.

I had known Bob for about six months and discovered through numerous conversations that he loved the world and what was in it. When it came to women, he often viewed them in ways that dishonored them and displeased God. Bob made it very clear that a woman's legs were very important. They were so important to him that he had an anklet that he used as a criterion for dating. Bob said that this anklet needed to fit around the woman's ankle in order for him to date her.

While viewing the next group moving from station to station he commented, "Now, there is a nice set of legs." Realizing that I was a light placed into Bob's life by the hand of my heavenly Father, I dismissed the idea of jumping up and pointing my finger at Bob and quoting Matthew 5:28: "But I say to you, that everyone who looks on a woman to lust for her has committed adultery with her already in his heart." On the other hand, what could I say? How could I share truth in such a way that it is not only heard but is seen as relevant? Some individuals just do not know what to say, so they pretend that they do not hear what is said or they quickly change the subject. But I responded by saying, "Yeah, you are right; those are a nice set of legs," because they were. Remembering that Bob appreciates humor, I proceeded to remove the watch from my wrist and in a humorous manner asked, "Bob, what is this?" He responded, "What? That? It's a watch!" I then asked Bob to tell me what he could discern about the maker of the watch by simply looking at it. He replied, "The watchmaker likes colors and he is interested in detail." I asked, "What is the watch used for?" He said, "To tell time, of course." I then inquired, "What would happen if I took this watch and used it to pound a nail into a wall?" While laughing, Bob replied, "You would break it!" "Why?" I asked. Bob quickly responded, "Because it wasn't made to pound nails into walls, ha ha!" I said, "You are correct, Bob, and as I think about the human body, it is beautiful. With and without clothing it was designed that way by God. But now mankind has abused the body, with adult and child pornography. It's sad, Bob, but we have taken something that was designed for beauty and appreciation and have perverted it." Bob looked up at me and said, "Ya know, I never thought about it that way."

God continued to deepen my relationship with Bob. This included Bob asking me questions about rooming with a woman, how to handle finances, how to respond to his parents, and many more common concerns. I would share the truth of Scripture with him, but never once did I hang a verse on the truth. I am not ashamed of the Gospel nor do I underestimate the power of God, but I have learned that if telling people the source of truth turns them away from listening to what I have to tell them, I do not feel compelled to say, "The Bible says." The intent is not to give the Bible credit for the source of truth, *the intent is to persuade them to draw closer to Christ.* You see, my intent was for Bob to see the relevancy of truth in his life and to recognize that all truth has its source in Christ, that all truth is God's truth.

Six months later, Bob came to me and asked, "Mike, where do you get all these good ideas?" I said, "Well, Bob, I attempt to live my life according to God's word; all the things I have been sharing with you are what I am learning from the Bible." Bob now wanted to study the Bible for himself. He had experienced the relevancy of biblical truth and now wanted more. The Spirit of God had drawn him closer to God. A few months later Bob became a Christian and is now growing deeply in his relationship with Christ.

There is nothing magical about situational teaching. Furthermore, I do not share this story as a cure-all or a formula to be employed without understanding the principles underlying situational teaching. Rather, this whole chapter is meant to give additional help to those who at times sense a bit of confusion as to how to facilitate someone's growth in Christ.

I have been playing racquetball with Tom for about three years. He is very much involved with materialism and attempts to find his worth in the accumulation of things. Recently while we were playing racquetball, I was about to serve, and when I checked to see if Tom was ready, he had his back to me while he watched an attractive woman walk by the court. He turned around and smiled and pointed while making hand gestures with reference to the shape of her body. I replied, "The real challenge in today's society is to look with appreciation without lusting." We both smiled and resumed play. Two weeks later we were playing again and a similar situation occurred. This time when Tom looked around at me he smiled, pointed, and said, "Just appreciating, just appreciating!" I simply replied, "Yes." We both laughed and resumed play. Tom had moved closer to Christ. In the one incident with Tom, I sowed truth by planting the idea that appreciation for beauty is healthy but lust is not. In the second, I watered that principle by agreeing with his statement of appreciation. Whether or not Tom becomes a Christian is up to God and Tom, but my role is clear and I will continue to love Tom as I sow and water in his life.

Our role includes facilitating a relational environment where the truth of Scripture can be relevantly understood. If this does take place through our friendships, then we can stimulate our friends to faith in Christ on the basis of the relevant information they have come to understand. Through this process we must pray and trust the Holy Spirit to continue to teach and convict others of their need for Christ. Authentic relationships with people take time. Meaningful participation in their lives includes knowing their uniqueness in each dimension of their humanity. We must be willing to empathize with them and to identify with them in the everyday common joys and struggles of life.

Relax, for God will bring these situations to pass; just continue to pursue God and maintain a prayerful eye on what the Holy Spirit is doing in other's lives and be a good listener. Remember, a common characteristic of Jesus' communication throughout the Gospels was that he started where people were in their lives and attempted to draw them closer to the Father. Study and compare Jesus' interactions with the woman at the well (John 4:7-38), Nicodemus (John 3), the adulterous women (John 8:1-11), and the rich young ruler (Mark 10:17-31). Jesus recognized where they were in life and drew them closer to the Father by helping them through an atmosphere of genuine love.

Where There Is a Will, There Is a Volitional Being

There is no guarantee that if we pray, live our Christian lives well before our co-workers, neighbors, or family members, and while praying, asking sincere questions and relating relevant stories, that they will ever come to know Christ. Then again, that is God's business, not ours. You and I have been called to be the light of the world regardless of the results. We need to remember our boundaries and three distinct but related roles:

1. We are lights and share truth via our lives and lips in relevant ways.

2. The Spirit of God convicts the world (and individuals) of sin, of righteousness, and of judgment.

3. Each individual can be enabled to choose Christ by the regenerating work of the Holy Spirit – this is God's work and not ours.

Theologians have argued for years over the priority and relationship of God's sovereignty and human will. I have found that the Scriptures teach that both are operative, but neither is emphasized at the expense of the other. The real problem is in our inability to reconcile these two truths which appear to be contradictory in the eyes of sinful and finite minds. The issues are that Scripture teaches that both are operative, and that, regardless, my role is not altered in reference to drawing people to Christ through planting and watering.

Direction Rather than Position

Charles Kraft points out our need to maintain a mentality of direction rather than of position:

> I would like to suggest that the basis on which God interacts with (and reveals himself to) human beings is what I will call a directional basis rather than a positional one [sic]. Faith/faithfulness is, of course, both the starting point and the sine qua non for a continuing relationship with God. But the Scriptures lead us to believe that those who, like the thief on the cross (Luke 23:42), simply reach out in faith at the last possible moment are as completely accepted by God as those who have expressed and developed their faith over decades. Jesus' illustration of the kingdom by the use of the story of the laborers who were all paid the same amount for unequal amounts of work (Matthew 20:1-16) would also seem to indicate that God has an attitude different from ours toward who is "in" and who is "out."[16]

Discipleship is a process rather than a product. For instance, maybe the person you are helping has had problems in the area of immorality. He may have averaged three sexual encounters per week. But since he is growing, he has two and soon only one per week. I do not mean to say that he is not sinning when he commits adultery, because he is. But there are very few individuals who, when snared in a sinful lifestyle, change overnight. Deep growth may very well be occurring within this person's life but the only visible outward expression is the decrease in his sexual encounters.

We need to focus on the practical aspects of holiness (which is a process) rather than on the position of holiness. Total holiness, the lack of all sin, in the everyday commonness of our individual lives will only be a reality after death. Scripture describes Christians as having already attained holiness in a positional sense. Yet all Christians are in the pursuit of holiness (direction); no one has obtained total holiness in the *practical* sense. There are no sinless Christians who have not experienced physical death. The only sinless Christians are in heaven. If you doubt this, ask any of your friends or family members if they think you are sinless. Old behaviors and habits do not usually change over night. Christians generally grow *slowly* in the manifestation of the Spirit's fruit. In the meantime, we must remember that ultimately God commands His children to love Him and their neighbors.

Summary

We realize that the two great commandments will grow (a process) in the lives of each individual in different ways and at different rates. Furthermore, God has given us examples of godly mentors in the present age for the children to imitate to facilitate their growth in the knowledge of Christ experientially. He has also given us the words of Scripture to be implanted and obeyed, and the principles of His Word to be internalized in order that we naturally trust Him and serve Him out of gratitude. God seems to be more interested in our motives and the process of growing in intimacy with Him than in our conformity to man-made rules and the absoluteness of our theology.

We must be content with our limitations in regard to our growth and the growth of others. Let us remember our role of planting and watering, and realize that God causes the growth and that He will bring people to maturity (Philippians 1:6).

Notes

[1] Conversation with the author.

[2] John V. Tailor quoted in Charles Kraft, *Christianity in Culture* (Maryknoll: Orbis Books, 1987), p. 279.

[3]Sharing information in relevant ways consists of communicating truth [accurate according to the intention of God] through a meaningful relationship in a way that your conversation partner is willing to listen and seriously consider what you are saying.

[4]Arthur F. Holmes *All Truth Is God's Truth* (Downers Grove: InterVarsity Press, 1977).

[5]Eddie Gibbs quoted in Derek Tidball, *The Social Context of the New Testament* (Grand Rapids: Zondervan Publishing House, 1984), p. 124.

[6]Ibid., p. 127.

[7]Dietrich Bonhoeffer, *The Cost of Discipleship* (London: SCM Press Ltd., 1959; reprinted New York: Touchstone Books, Simon & Schuster Inc., 1995), p. 37.

[8]Tidball, p. 112.

[9]Paul Hiebert, *Anthropological Insights for Missionaries* (Grand Rapids: Baker Book House, 1985), p. 24.

[10]Ibid., p. 26.

[11]Conversation with the author.

[12]Conversation with the author.

[13]Hiebert, p. 161, citing Jack Dabner, *Notes on Communication* (Singapore: Haggai Institute, 1983), p. 4.

[14]Conversation with the author.

[15]Hiebert, p. 269.

[16]Kraft, p. 240.

Review – Section Three

This section examined how our role as Christians in ministry must be distinguished from the convicting work of the Holy Spirit as does our role in helping others acknowledge and live in the presence of God. The fruit of the Holy Spirit – "love, joy, peace, patience, kindness, goodness, faithfulness, gentleness, self-control" etc. (Galatians 5:22-23) – are the supernatural produce of one's abiding in Christ, they are not the result of trying to be righteous or of trying to act appropriately.

We also saw that there are various stages of spiritual development each Christian goes through and some common characteristics and misunderstandings we have as we grow in knowing Christ. The Holy Spirit moves people through the growth process, in light of individual temperament, talents, abilities and call of God. God causes people to grow; our role is to help create a relational environment for others' growth and avoid being stumbling blocks.

By becoming students of others we seek to serve and by understanding the overall growth process, we can minister to others in timely and relevant ways. Through *abiding in Christ* and by taking advantage of ministry opportunities we will grow into what God designed us to be and do.

This is truly the life I want in Christ.

Summary

Section One of this book focused upon the darkness of humanity's problem. We are created and designed by God as spiritual beings with physical, moral, volitional, emotional, relational, and rational dimensions. The depth and breadth of Adam's fall touched all of who and what we are. We are not in our worst possible state, but all of whom and what we are is certainly marred by sin.

Section Two gave us a ray of light. We learned that Jesus' remedy for humanity's sin problem is whole-person in nature. We need to be set free, and experiencing truth is vitally linked to that freedom. When Jesus said, "It is finished" (John 19:30), Satan was utterly defeated. The nature of the Church is to attack the gates of Hell. Since non-Christians are spiritually both blind and in bondage to sin, Christians need to go to them with the good news of Jesus.

We examined the holiness of God and saw that it is only through God's holiness that we can experience freedom. God presents the opportunity for freedom through knowing His Son experientially, the answer to our depravity. Others throughout history have walked closely with God and we saw from them practical ways for abiding in Christ.

Section Three focused upon growth. In order for individual Christians and the Church to grow, clearly defined roles must be understood and lived out. The convicting role of the Holy Spirit and the Christian's role of light-bearing work hand-in-hand in ministry. But we Christians are prone to forget our role and sometimes erroneously attempt to assume the role of the Holy Spirit. Spiritual growth is developmental and we must move from being babes in Christ to becoming children, then young adults, and on to mature adulthood. Keeping the focus of growth central, we investigated practical ways to plant and water among both the non-Christians and Christians, through situational teaching, highlighting the use of relevant questions and storytelling.

Main Points to Remember

In outline fashion, the following are the important components of this book.

1. Realize that individuals are "totally depraved," yet be a student of them. Prayerfully examine the dimensions of their lives with the intent of learning their uniqueness among God's creation.

2. Trust God to use you in their lives, but be willing to enter into their individual worldviews and cultures; do not demand or expect them to live in or according to your Christian worldview and culture.

3. Pray for insight into what the Holy Spirit is already doing in their lives. Discern what the Holy Spirit is convicting them of, and through your relationship and situational teaching, provide an environment for them to experience the relevancy of God's Word.

4. Anticipate that the Holy Spirit will continue to convict people of sin, of righteousness, and of judgment. Trust that the Holy Spirit will link His convicting work within the individual's conscience through your example, the verses of Scripture, and the principles of God's Word.

5. Avoid making the spiritual disciplines ends in themselves or means to an end. Christ is our focus not any activity regardless of how holy it may appear.

6. Teach Christians how to imitate godly models, help them to implant the verses of God's Word into their hearts, and how to internalize the principles of Scripture in relevant ways. A key to relevancy is that the means and strategies do not draw attention to themselves, but rather the emphasis is on knowing Christ and abiding in His presence. If in your attempt to help people abide in Christ, your methods draw attention to themselves, then your strategy has become an end in itself, a stumbling block. We are not calling people to programs, paradigms, strategies, means, or methods, but to intimacy with Christ.

7. Remember that the Great Commission naturally grows out of the reality of the Great Commandment experienced in your life.

8. The intent of discipleship is to help people abide in Christ in all of who they are (being) and in all of what they do (experience).

When Everything Is Said and Done . . .

The importance for *whole-person* discipleship cannot be overemphasized. The first Christians, coming out of a pagan society, were entrenched in thought patterns, attitudes, values, and beliefs that were incongruent with the Word of God. These new believers needed not only to hear what was right, but to see a whole-person model in action. Christian truth presented verbally while necessary, was inadequate for the needs at hand. These new children of God needed to observe truth embodied in the whole-person lives of those who promoted these truths. Jesus, the Apostles, Paul, and others were conscious of their responsibility to give young believers solid biblical truth, yet they were also keenly aware of the need to give clear, practical, and tangible proof embodied in their own lives. They had a keen interest in seeing others live lives of freedom and peace in reconciliation with God.

Peace and freedom are two of the greatest gifts we possess in Christ, which rightly understood, can stimulate the desire to disciple others. Whole-person discipleship requires the discipler to be a kingdom broker. We live, in a sense, between two kingdoms. We must transfer truth from God's kingdom to the victims of the kingdom of darkness. This transfer applies to both Christian and non-Christian alike, because anytime a Christian sins, for that moment, he is acting as a member of the kingdom of darkness. Whole-person discipleship emphasizes kingdom living, light, in all six dimensions of a person.

When Jesus entered human history, He revealed more of what his kingdom entails. His kingdom is present and will be fully recognized and realized at Jesus' second coming. The kingdom of God is upon us now, our bondage to sin is broken, and freedom can be realized as we turn to the one and true liberator – Jesus Christ.

Liberation from sin is possible; let us help people discover what the Savior meant when He declared – "It is finished." This liberation is not meant only for the future also but for the present. The Church's responsibility is to be the vehicle of liberation between the first and second comings of Christ. Peace, joy, and fruitful abundant living is free and offered to all. Our job as kingdom brokers is to help people discover this liberation and how to live within its freedom. This view of spiritual development involves not only forgiveness of sins, but also the power to live in light of our redemption in Christ. Living in and acknowledging the presence of God (abiding in Christ) must be central to discipleship. Discipleship cannot occur without the disciplemaker abiding in Christ also.

In order to help fulfill the Great Commission, we must not be satisfied in training people in one or two dimensions of our humanity. Rather, we must imitate both Jesus and Paul in their use of whole-person discipleship emphasizing the core characteristic of discipleship: holiness.

Since humanity is totally depraved, true discipleship is not satisfied with people merely having the right ideas about God. We are designed to not only love God with all our heart, soul, mind, and strength, but also to help others do the same.

God is the thesis of abundant life,
humanity is the antithesis of abundant life,
Christ is the synthesis for abundant life.
"Cease striving and know that I am God."
— Psalm 46:10 —

Appendix A: Bible Passages Related to Our Rational Dimension

The following references are divided into categories relating to the rational dimension of our humanity. In the Bible "heart" often refers to the rational or central decision making aspect of our being.

Commitment to God

Deuteronomy 6:5 (cited in Matthew 22:37, Mark 12:30, and Luke 10:27) You shall love the LORD your God with all your heart, and with all your soul, and with all your mind.

1 Kings 8:61 Let your heart therefore be wholly devoted to the LORD our God, to walk in His statutes and to keep His commandments, as at this day.

1 Kings 11:4 For it came about when Solomon was old, his wives turned his heart away after other gods; and his heart was not wholly devoted to the LORD his God, as the heart of David his father had been.

Isaiah 26:3 The steadfast of mind Thou wilt keep in perfect peace, because he trusts in Thee.

Deception

Jeremiah 17:9 The heart is more deceitful than all else and is desperately sick; who can understand it?

2 Corinthians 4:4 ... the god of this world has blinded the minds of the unbelieving, that they may not see....

1 Timothy 6:5 ... and constant friction between men of depraved mind and deprived of the truth....

2 Timothy 3:8 And just as Jannes and Jambres opposed Moses, so these men also oppose the truth, men of depraved mind, rejected in regard to the faith.

Titus 1:15 ... but both their mind and their conscience are defiled.

Instruction/Direction

Psalm 16:7 I will bless the LORD who has counseled me; indeed, my mind instructs me in the night.

Proverbs 16:9 The mind of a man plans his way but the LORD directs his steps.

Proverbs 17:20 He who has a crooked mind finds no good, and he who is perverted in his language falls into evil.

Ecclesiastes 7:4 The mind of the wise is in the house of mourning, while the mind of fools is in the house of pleasure.

Daniel 1:8 But Daniel made up his mind that he would not defile himself with the king's choice food....

Mark 7:21 For from within, out of the heart of men, proceed the evil thoughts, fornications, thefts, murders, adulteries....

Mark 8:33 [Jesus] rebuked Peter, and said, "Get behind Me, Satan; for you are not setting your mind on God's interests, but on man's."

Romans 8:6-7 For the mind set on the flesh is death, but the mind set on the Spirit is life and peace, because the mind set on the flesh is hostile toward God; for it does not subject itself to the law of God, for it is not even able to do so.

Romans 12:2-3 And do not be conformed to this world, but be transformed by the renewing of your mind, that you may prove what the will of God is, that which is good and acceptable and perfect....I say every man among you not to think more highly of himself than he ought to think, but to think so as to have sound judgment....

Romans 12:16 Be of the same mind toward one another; do not be haughty in mind, but associate with the lowly. Do not be wise in your own estimation.

Ephesians 2:3... indulging the desires of the flesh and of the mind ....

Colossians 1:21 And although you were formerly alienated and hostile in mind, engaged in evil deeds....

Colossians 3:2 Set your mind on the things above, not on the things that are on earth.

Knowledge/Content
Proverbs 15:14 The mind of the intelligent seeks knowledge, but the mouth of fools feeds on folly.

Proverbs 18:15 The mind of the prudent acquires knowledge, and the ear of the wise seeks knowledge.

Proverbs 22:17 Incline your ear and hear the words of the wise, and apply your mind to my knowledge;

Proverbs 23:7 For as he thinks within himself, so he is.

Philippians 4:8-9 Finally, brethren, whatever is true, whatever is honorable, whatever is right, whatever is pure, whatever is lovely, whatever is of good repute, if there is any excellence and if anything worthy of praise, let your mind dwell on these things. The things you have learned and received and heard and seen in me, practice these things; and the God of peace shall be with you.

Hebrews 10:16 (citing Jeremiah 31:33) This is the covenant that I will make with them after those days, says the Lord: I will put my laws upon their heart, and upon their mind I will write them....

Being of One/the Same Mind
Romans 15:5 Now [God] grant you to be of the same mind....

1 Corinthians 1:10 ... you be made complete in the same mind....

1 Corinthians 2:16 ... we have the mind of Christ.

Philippians 1:27... you are standing firm in one spirit, with one mind striving together for the faith of the gospel.

Philippians 2:2 Make my joy complete by being of the same mind....

Testing by God

Psalm 26:2 Examine me, O LORD, and try me; test my mind and my heart.

Jeremiah 17:10 I, the LORD, search the heart, I test the mind....

Jeremiah 20:12 Yet, O LORD of hosts, Thou who dost test the righteous, who seest the mind and the heart . . . .

Understanding

Job 38:36 Who has put wisdom in the inner most being? Or has given understanding to the mind?

Proverbs 12:8 A man will be praised according to his insight, but one of perverse mind will be despised.

Proverbs 18:2 A fool does not delight in understanding, but only in revealing his mind.

Ecclesiastes 7:25 I directed my mind to know, to investigate, and to seek wisdom and an explanation, and to know the evil of folly and the foolishness of madness.

Isaiah 1:18 Come now, and let us reason together, says the Lord....

Romans 1:21... but they became futile in their speculations, and their foolish heart was darkened.

Romans 1:28 And just as they did not see fit to acknowledge God any longer, God gave them over to a depraved mind, to do those things which are not proper.

Ephesians 4:17-18 Gentiles walk in the futility of their mind, being darkened in their understanding, excluded from the life of God, because of the ignorance that is in them ...

Ephesians 4:23. . . be renewed in the spirit of your mind . . . .

Philippians 2:3 . . . but with humility of mind let each of you . . . .

Colossians 2:18 . . . inflated without cause by his fleshly mind . . . .

Appendix B: Bible Passages Related to Our Physical Dimension

The following references are divided in categories showing Jesus' concern for healing people He encountered as recorded in the Gospels and Paul's emphasis on the human body.

Jesus Cast Out Demons/Unclean Spirits

Matthew

8:16 – many who were brought to Him (at Peter's home)

8:28-34 – two men from the tombs in the country of the Gadarenes

9:32-33 – a mute man

10:8 – report to John the Baptist demons are cast out

12:22 – a blind and mute man

15:21-28 – a Canaanite (Syrophoenician) woman's daughter

Mark

1:23-28 – man with an unclean spirit in the synagogue at Capernaum

1:32-34 – many who were brought to Him (at Peter's home)

1:39 – in the synagogues throughout all Galilee

3:10-12 – many with unclean spirits at the seaside

5:1-13 – Gerasene demoniac

7:24-30 – Syrophoenician woman's daughter with an unclean spirit

9:14-27 – man's son who had convulsions from an unclean ("deaf and mute") spirit which the disciples could not cast out

Luke

4:33-35 – spirit of an unclean demon

4:41 – demons cast out

6:18-19 – unclean spirits cast out

7:21 – evil spirits cast out

8:2 – evil spirits cast out

8:26-36 – demoniac cured

9:38-43 – spirit possessed boy

11:14-15 – mute demon

Jesus Provided Food for the Hungry
Matthew
14:14-21 – fed five thousand
15:32-38 – fed four thousand

Mark
6:37-44 – fed five thousand
8:1-9 – fed four thousand

Luke 9:12-17 – fed five thousand

John 6:1-14 – fed five thousand

Jesus Raised the Dead
Matthew
9:18-25 – synagogue official's daughter
10:8 – commissioned the twelve disciples to raise the dead
11:5 – report to John the Baptist the dead are raised

Mark 5:35-43 – synagogue official's daughter

Luke
7:11-17 – widow's only son
7:22 – report to John the Baptist the dead are raised
8:49-56 – synagogue official's daughter

John 11:1-47 – Lazarus

Jesus Cured Sickness and Disease
Matthew
4:23-24 – all kinds of sickness
8:1-4 – leper
8:5-13 – paralyzed servant of the centurion
8:15 – fever – Peter's mother-in-law
9:1-7 – paralytic
9:20-22 – woman's hemorrhage

9:27-30 – two blind men
9:32-33 – mute man
9:35 – every kind of disease and sickness
10:8 – sick and lepers
11:5 – blind, lame, lepers, deaf
12:9-13 – withered hand
12:15 – healed them all
12:22 – blind and mute
14:14 – healed sick
14:35-36 - sick
15:29-31 - lame, crippled, blind, mute, etc.
17:14-18 - lunatic
19:2 - healed them
20:29-34 - blind
21:14 - blind and lame

Mark
1:29-31 – fever
1:32-34 – ill
1:40-42 – leper
2:3-12 – paralytic
3:1-5 – withered hand
3:10-12 – healed many
5:25-34 – woman's hemorrhage
6:5 – healed sick
6:53-56 – healed sick
7:31-37– deaf and mute
8:22-26 – blind
10:46-52 – blind Bartimaeus

Luke
4:38-39 – fever
4:40 – various diseases
5:12-13 – leper
5:18-26 – paralytic
6:6-11 – withered hand

6:18-19 – various diseases

7:1-10 – sick slave of Centurion

7:21 – various diseases, afflictions, blind

7:22 – blind, lame, lepers, deaf, etc.

8:2 – various sicknesses

8:43-47 – woman's hemorrhage

9:11 – healed the needy

13:10-13 – woman bent double/over

14:1-4 – dropsy

17:11-14 – ten lepers

18:35-43 – blind

John

4:46-54 – sick son of nobleman

5:5-9 – sick man

9:1-7 – blind

Jesus Protected/Saved People from Death

Luke

8:22-25 – saved from storm

Paul

The apostle Paul also recognized the importance of keeping a healthy body. He viewed keeping one's body pure and holy as a matter of stewardship.

Use the Body to Honor God

Romans 6:13

... and do not go on presenting the members of your body to sin as instruments of unrighteousness; but present yourselves to God as those alive from the dead, and your members as instruments of righteousness to God.

1 Corinthians 6:13, 18, and 20

Food is for the stomach, and the stomach is for food; but God will do away with both of them. Yet the body is not for immorality, but for the Lord; and the Lord is for the body.... Flee immorality. Every other sin that a man commits is outside the body, but the immoral man sins against his own body.... For you have been bought with a price: therefore glorify God in your body.

God's Temple

1 Corinthians 3:16-17
Do you not know that you are a temple of God, and that the Spirit of God dwells in you? If any man destroys the temple of God, God will destroy him, for the temple of God is holy, and that is what you are.

2 Corinthians 6:16
What agreement has the temple of God with idols? For we are the temple of the living God; just as God said, "I will dwell in them and walk among them; and I will be their God, and they shall be my people."

Appendix C: Bible Passages Related to
Our Moral Dimension

The following references are divided into categories related to the moral dimension of our humanity.

Disobeying God's Commandments, Statutes, etc.
Exodus 16:28 – Then the Lord said to Moses, "How long do you refuse to keep My commandments and My instructions?"

2 Kings 17:19 – Also Judah did not keep the commandments of the Lord their God, but walked in the customs which Israel had introduced.

2 Chronicles 24:20 – Thus God has said, "Why do you transgress the commandments of the Lord and do not prosper? Because you have forsaken the Lord, He has also forsaken you."

Ezra 9:10-11 – And now, our God, what shall we say after this? For we have forsaken Thy commandments, which Thou hast commanded by Thy servants the prophets...

Isaiah 48:18 – If only you had paid attention to My commandments! Then your well-being would have been like a river, and your righteousness like the waves of the sea.

Daniel 9:5 –... we have sinned, committed iniquity, acted wickedly, and rebelled, even turning aside from Thy commandments and ordinances.

God's Commandments
Exodus 20/Deuteronomy 5 – The Ten Commandments

Obeying God's Commandments, Statutes, etc.
Genesis 26:4-5 – I will multiply your descendants... because Abraham obeyed Me and kept My charge, My commandments, My statutes and my Laws.

Exodus 15:26 – And He said, "If you will give earnest heed to the voice of the Lord your God, and do what is right in His sight, and give ear to His commandments, and keep all His statutes, I will...."

Exodus 20:6 –... but showing lovingkindness to thousands, to those who love Me and keep My commandments.

Leviticus 22:31 – So you shall keep My commandments, and do them.

Numbers 15:39 – And it shall be a tassel for you to look at and remember all the commandments of the Lord, so as to do them and not follow after your own heart and your own eyes, after which you played the harlot.

Joshua 22:5 – Only be very careful to observe the commandments and the law which Moses the servant of the Lord commanded you, to love the Lord your God and walk in all His ways and keep His commandments and hold fast to Him and serve Him will all your heart and with all your soul.

Judges 22:17 – They turned aside quickly from the way in which their fathers had walked in obeying the commandments of the Lord; they did not do as their fathers.

1 Kings 6:12 – Concerning this house which you are building, if you will walk in My statutes and execute My ordinances and keep all My commandments by walking in them, then I will carry out My word with you which I spoke to David your father.

1 Chronicles 29:19 – ... and give to my son Solomon a perfect heart to keep Thy commandments, Thy testimonies, and Thy statutes, and to do them all, and to build the temple, for which I have made provision.

Nehemiah 1:5 –... for those who love Him and keep His commandments...

Psalm 1 – Psalm 1 emphasizes the joys and benefits of those whose way is to delight in and meditate on the law of the Lord in contrast to the ways of the wicked.

Psalm 19 – Psalm 19 celebrates the works and Word of God and the benefits of knowing and obeying the law of the Lord.

Psalm 119 – Psalm 119 celebrates the joys and benefits of knowing and obeying the law of the Lord.

Proverbs 4:4 – Then He taught me and said to me, "Let your heart hold fast my words; keep my commandments and live . . ."

Proverbs 29:18 – Where there is no vision, the people are unrestrained, but happy is he who keeps the law.

Ecclesiastes 12:13 – The conclusion, when all has been heard, is; fear God and keep His commandments, because this applies to every person.

Matthew 22:37-40 – . . .'You shall love the LORD your God with all your heart, and with all your soul, and with all your mind.' This is the great and foremost commandment. The second is like it, 'You shall love your neighbor as yourself.'

Luke 1:6 – And they were both righteous in the sight of God, walking blamelessly in all the commandments and requirements of the Lord.

John 14:21 – He who has My commandments and keeps them, he it is who loves Me; and he who loves Me shall be loved by My Father, and I will love him, and will disclose Myself to him.

1 Corinthians 7:19 – Circumcision is nothing, and uncircumcision is nothing, but what matters is the keeping of the commandments of God.

1 John 2:3 – And by this we know that we have come to know Him, if we keep His commandments.

2 John 1:6 – And this is love, that we walk according to His commandments. This is the commandment, just as you have heard from the beginning, that you should walk in it.

Revelation 12:17 – And the dragon was enraged with the woman, and went off to make war with the rest of her offspring, who keep the commandments of God and hold to the testimony of Jesus.

Remembering God's Commandments, Statutes, etc.

Numbers 15:39 – And it shall be a tassel for you to look at and remember all the commandments of the LORD, so as to do them and not follow after your own heart and your own eyes, after which you played the harlot.

Joshua 1:8 – This book of the law shall not depart from your mouth, but you shall meditate on it day and night, so that you may be careful to do according to all that is written in it; for then you will make your way prosperous, and then you will have success.

Teaching God's Commandments, Statutes, etc.

Deuteronomy 6:6-7 – And these words, which I am commanding you today, shall be on your heart; and you shall teach them diligently to your sons and shall talk of them when you sit in your house and when you walk by the way and when you lie down and when you rise up.

Ezra 7:9-10 –. . . because the good hand of the Lord was upon him. For Ezra had set his heart to study the law of the Lord, and to practice it, and to teach His statutes and ordinances in Israel.

2 Timothy 3:16-17 – All Scripture is inspired by God and profitable for teaching, for reproof, for correction, for training in righteousness; that the man of God may be adequate for every good work.

2 Timothy 2:2 – And the things which you have heard from me in the presence of many witnesses, these entrust to faithful men, who will be able to teach others.

Appendix D: Bible Passages Related to
Our Volitional Dimension

The following references are divided into categories related to the volitional dimension of our humanity.

Watching
Proverbs 4:23 – Watch over your heart with all diligence, for from it flow springs of life.

Wishing/Doing
Matthew 19:21-22 – Jesus said to him, "If you wish to be complete, go and sell your possessions and give to the poor, and you shall have treasure in heaven; and come, follow me."

Romans 7:15-20 – For that which I am doing, I do not understand; for I am not practicing what I would like to do, but I am doing the very thing I hate. But if I do the very thing I do not wish to do, I agree with the Law, confessing that it is good. So now, no longer am I the one doing it, but sin which indwells me. For I know that nothing good dwells in me, that is, in my flesh; for the wishing is present in me, but the doing of the good is not. For the good that I wish, I do not do; but I practice the very evil that I do not wish. But if I am doing the very thing I do not wish, I am no longer the one doing it, but sin which dwells in me.

1 Corinthians 10:13 – No temptation has overtaken you but such as is common to man; and God is faithful, who will not allow you to be tempted beyond what you are able, but with the temptation will provide the way of escape also, that you may be able to endure it.

Willing
1 Chronicles 28:9 – . . . and serve Him with a whole heart and a willing mind; for the Lord searches all hearts, and understands every intent of the thoughts . . . .

Set and Let
Romans 8:5-8 – For those who are according to the flesh set their minds on the things of the flesh, but those who are according to the Spirit, the things of the Spirit. For the

mind set on the flesh is death, but the mind set on the Spirit is life and peace, because the mind set on the flesh is hostile toward God; for it does not subject itself to the law of God, for it is not even able to do so; and those who are in the flesh cannot please God.

Ephesians 4:29 – Let no unwholesome word proceed from your mouth . . .

Philippians 4:8 – . . . let your mind dwell on these things.

Colossians 3:2 – Set your mind on the things above, not on the things that are on earth.

Putting On/Aside

Colossians 3:8 – But now you also, put them all aside: anger, wrath, ...

Colossians 3:12-14 – And so, as those who have been chosen of God, holy and beloved, put on a heart of compassion, kindness, humility, gentleness and patience; bearing with one another, and forgiving each other, whoever has a complaint against anyone; just as the Lord forgave you, so also should you. And beyond all these things put on love, which is the perfect bond of unity.

Appendix E: Bible Passages Related to Our Emotional Dimension

The following references are divided into categories related to the emotional dimension of our humanity.

Anger/Jealousy

Proverbs 29:22 – An angry man stirs up strife, and a hot-tempered man abounds in transgression.

Matthew 18:34 – And his lord, moved with anger, handed him over to the torturers until he should repay all that was owed him.

Mark 3:5 – And after looking around at them with anger, grieved at their hardness of heart, He said to the man, "Stretch out your hand." And he stretched it out, and his hand was restored.

Matthew 5:22 – But I say to you that everyone who is angry with his brother shall be guilty before the court . . . .

Luke 14:21 – And the slave came back and reported this to his master. Then the head of the household became angry and said to his slave, 'Go out at once into the streets and lanes of the city and bring in here the poor and crippled and blind and lame.'

Luke 15:28 – But he became angry, and was not willing to go in; and his father came out and began entreating him.

John 7:23 – . . . are you angry with Me because I made an entire man well on the Sabbath?

Acts 12:20 – Now he was very angry with the people of Tyre and Sidon . . . .

Ephesians 4:26 – Be angry, and yet do not sin; do not let the sun go down on your anger.

1 Corinthians 13:4-7 – Love is patient, love is kind, and is not jealous; love does not brag and is not arrogant, does not act unbecomingly; it does not seek its own, is not provoked, does not take into account a wrong suffered, does not rejoice in unrighteousness, but rejoices with the truth.

Hebrews 3:17 – And with whom was He angry for forty years? Was it not with those who sinned, whose bodies fell in the wilderness?

Anxiety/Distress
1 Samuel 1:10 – And she, greatly distressed, prayed to the Lord and wept bitterly.

Isaiah 41:10 – Do not fear, for I am with you; do not anxiously look about you, for I am your God. I will strengthen you, surely I will help you, surely I will uphold you with My righteous right hand.

Philippians 4:6-7 – Be anxious for nothing, but in everything by prayer and supplication with thanksgiving let your requests be made known to God. And the peace of God, which surpasses all comprehension, shall guard your hearts and your minds in Christ Jesus.

Courage/Encouraged
Acts 27:22 – And yet now I urge you to keep up your courage, for there shall be no loss of life among you, but only of the ship.

Acts 27:25 – Therefore, keep up your courage, men, for I believe God, that it will turn out exactly as I have been told.

Acts 27:36 – And all of them were encouraged, and they themselves also took food.

Fear/Trembling
Isaiah 41:10 – Do not fear, for I am with you; do not anxiously look about you, for I am your God. I will strengthen you, surely I will help you, surely I will uphold you with My righteous right hand.

Philippians 2:12 – So then, my beloved, just as you have always obeyed, not as in my presence only, but now much more in my absence, work out your salvation with fear and trembling.

Joy/Rejoicing/Thankfulness/Peace

Romans 15:13 – Now may the God of hope fill you with all joy and peace in believing, that you may abound in hope by the power of the Holy Spirit.

1 Corinthians 13:4-7 – Love is patient, love is kind, and is not jealous; love does not brag and is not arrogant, does not act unbecomingly; it does not seek its own, is not provoked, does not take into account a wrong suffered, does not rejoice in unrighteousness, but rejoices with the truth.

Philippians 4:6-7 – Be anxious for nothing, but in everything by prayer and supplication with thanksgiving let your requests be made known to God. And the peace of God, which surpasses all comprehension, shall guard your hearts and your minds in Christ Jesus.

1 Thessalonians 5:16-18 – Rejoice always; pray without ceasing; in everything give thanks; for this is God's will for you in Christ Jesus.

Provoke/Irritate

1 Samuel 1:6 – Her rival, however, would provoke her bitterly to irritate her, because the Lord had closed her womb.

1 Corinthians 13:4-7 – Love is patient, love is kind, and is not jealous; love does not brag and is not arrogant, does not act unbecomingly; it does not seek its own, is not provoked, does not take into account a wrong suffered, does not rejoice in unrighteousness, but rejoices with the truth.

Ephesians 6:4 – And fathers, do not provoke your children to anger, but bring them up in the discipline and instruction of the Lord.

Sullen/Grieved/Sad

1 Samuel 1:18 – . . . and her face was no longer sad.

Mark 3:5 – And after looking around at them with anger, grieved at their hardness of heart, He said to the man, "Stretch out your hand." And he stretched it out, and his hand was restored.

1 Kings 21:4 – So Ahab came into his house sullen and vexed . . . .

Wept/Stirred

Genesis 43:30 – And Joseph hurried out for he was deeply stirred over his brother, and he sought a place to weep; and he entered his chamber and wept there.

Genesis 45:1 – Then Joseph could not control himself before all those who stood by him, and he cried, "Have everyone go out from me." So there was no man with him when Joseph made himself known to his brothers. And he wept so loudly that the Egyptians heard it, and the household of Pharaoh heard of it.

1 Samuel 1:10 – And she, greatly distressed, prayed to the Lord and wept bitterly.

John 11:35 – Jesus wept.

Appendix F: Bible Passages Related to
Our Relational Dimension

The following references are divided into categories related to the relational dimension of our humanity.

God

Proverbs 3:5-6 – Trust in the Lord with all your heart, and do not lean on your own understanding. In all your ways acknowledge Him, and He will make your paths straight.

Proverbs 29:25 – The fear of man brings a snare, but he who trusts in the Lord will be exalted.

Matthew 22:37-38 – You shall love the LORD your God with all your heart, and with all your soul, and with all your mind. This is the great and foremost commandment.

John 3:16 – For God so loved the world, that He gave His only begotten Son, that whoever believes in Him should not perish, but have eternal life.

John 13:34-35 – A new commandment I give to you, that you love one another, even as I have loved you, that you also love one another. By this all men will know that you are My disciples, if you have love for one another.

Romans 8:35-39 – Who shall separate us from the love of Christ? . . . nor height, nor depth, nor any other created thing, shall be able to separate us from the love of God, which is in Christ Jesus our Lord.

1 John 4:19 – We love, because He first loved us.

Self

Proverbs 3:5-6 – Trust in the LORD with all your heart, and do not lean on your own understanding. In all your ways acknowledge Him, and He will make your paths straight.

Proverbs 3:7 – Do not be wise in your own eyes; Fear the Lord and turn from evil.

Matthew 22:39 – The second is like it, You shall love your neighbor as yourself.

Romans 8:23 – And not only this, but also we ourselves, having the first fruits of the Spirit, even we ourselves groan within ourselves, waiting eagerly for our adoption as sons, the redemption of our body.

Romans 13:9 – For this, "You shall not commit adultery, you shall not murder, you shall not steal, you shall not covet," and if there is any other commandment, it is summed up in this saying, "You shall love your neighbor as yourself."

Others

Proverbs 29:7 – The righteous is concerned for the rights of the poor, the wicked does not understand *such* concern.

Proverbs 29:14 – If a king judges the poor with truth, his throne will be established forever.

Proverbs 29:25 – The fear of man brings a snare, but he who trusts in the Lord will be exalted.

Matthew 19:19 – Honor your father and mother; and You shall love your neighbor as yourself.

Matthew 22:39 – The second is like it, You shall love your neighbor as yourself.

Luke 22:17-22 – And when He had taken a cup and given thanks He said, "Take this and share it among yourselves . . . ." And when He had taken some bread and given thanks, He broke it, and gave it to them, saying, "This is My body which is given for you; do this in remembrance of Me."

John 13:34-35 – A new commandment I give to you, that you love one another, even as I have loved you, that you also love one another. By this all men will know that you are My disciples, if you have love for one another.

Romans 12:13 – . . . contributing to the needs of the saints, practicing hospitality.

Romans 13:1 – Let every person be in subjection to the governing authorities. For there is no authority except from God, and those which exist are established by God.

Romans 13:7-9 – Render to all what is due them: tax to whom tax is due; custom to whom custom; fear to whom fear; honor to whom honor. Owe nothing to anyone except to love one another; for he who loves his neighbor has fulfilled the law. For this, "You shall not commit adultery, you shall not murder, you shall not steal, you shall not covet," and if there is any other commandment, it is summed up in this saying, "You shall love your neighbor as yourself."

Romans 14:13 – Therefore let us not judge one another anymore, but rather determine this – not to put an obstacle or a stumbling block in a brothers way.

1 Corinthians 1:10 – Now I exhort you, brethren, by the name of our Lord Jesus Christ, that you all agree, and there be no divisions among you, but you be made complete in the same mind and in the same judgment.

1 Corinthians 4:6. – . . . that in us you might learn not to exceed what is written, in order that no one of you might become arrogant on behalf of one against the other.

1 Corinthians 5:13 – But those who are outside, God judges. Remove the wicked man from among yourselves.

1 Corinthians 6:1,7 – Does any one of you, when he has a case against his neighbor, dare to go to law before the unrighteous, and not before the saints? . . . Actually, then, it is already a defeat for you, that you have lawsuits with one another. Why not rather be wronged? Why not rather be defrauded?

Ephesians 4:32 – And be kind to one another, tender-hearted, forgiving each other, just as God in Christ also has forgiven you.

1 Thessalonians 5:14 – And we urge you, brethren, admonish the unruly, encourage the fainthearted, help the weak, be patient with all men.

1 John 4:19 – We love, because He first loved us.

Creation

Genesis 1:28 – And God blessed them; and God said to them, "Be fruitful and multiply, and fill the earth, and subdue it; and rule over the fish of the sea and over the birds of the sky, and over every living thing that moves on the earth."

Genesis 2:15 – Then the Lord God took the man and put him into the garden of Eden to cultivate it and keep it.

Romans 8:19-22 – For the anxious longing of the creation waits eagerly for the revealing of the sons of God. For the creation was subjected to futility, not of its own will, but because of Him who subjected it, in hope that the creation itself also will be set free from its slavery to corruption into the freedom of the glory of the children of God. For we know that the whole creation groans and suffers the pains of childbirth together until now.

Appendix G: Bible Passages Related to Abiding

The following are divided into categories related to abiding.

Abiding in God, in the Father, in Christ

Psalm 15:1 – O Lord, who may abide in Thy tent? Who may dwell on Thy holy hill?

Psalm 91:1 – He who dwells in the shelter of the Most High will abide in the shadow of the Almighty.

John 15:4 – Abide in me, and I in you. As the branch cannot bear fruit of itself, unless it abides in the vine, so neither can you, unless you abide in Me.

John 15:6-7 – If anyone does not abide in Me, he is thrown away as a branch, and dries up; and they gather them, and cast them into the fire, and they are burned. If you abide in Me, and My words abide in you, ask whatever you wish, and it shall be done for you.

Romans 8:1 – There is therefore now no condemnation for those who are in Christ Jesus.

2 Corinthians 10:5 – We are destroying speculations and every lofty thing raised up against the knowledge of God, and we are taking every thought captive to the obedience of Christ.

1 John 2:6 – The one who says he abides in Him ought himself to walk in the same manner as He walked.

1 John 2:24, 27-28 – As for you, let that abide in you which you heard from the beginning. If what you heard from the beginning abides in you, you also will abide in the Son and in the Father. . . . and just as it has taught you, you abide in Him. And now, little children, abide in Him . . . .

1 John 3:6 – No one who abides in Him sins . . . .

1 John 3:24 – And the one who keeps His commandments abides in Him, and He in him. And we know by this that He abides in us, by the Spirit who He has given us.

1 John 4:13, 15-16 – By this we know that we abide in Him and He in us, because He has given us of His Spirit. . . . Whoever confesses that Jesus is the Son of God, God abides in him, and he in God. . . . God is love, and the one who abides in love abides in God, and God abides in him.

Christ Abiding in Us

John 15:4-5 – Abide in me, and I in you. As the branch cannot bear fruit of itself, unless it abides in the vine, so neither can you, unless you abide in Me. I am the vine, you are the branches; he who abides in Me, and I in him, he bears much fruit; for apart from Me you can do nothing.

1 John 3:24 – And the one who keeps His commandments abides in Him, and He in him. And we know by this that He abides in us, by the Spirit who He has given us.

1 John 4:12-13, 15-16 – No one has beheld God at any time; if we love one another, God abides in us, and His love is perfected in us. By this we know that we abide in Him and He in us, because He has given us of His Spirit. . . . Whoever confesses that Jesus is the Son of God, God abides in him, and he in God. God is love, and the one who abides in love abides in God, and God abides in him.

Abiding in His Word/Truth/Love/Light

John 5:38 – And you do not have His word abiding in you, for you do not believe Him whom He sent.

John 8:31 – If you abide in My word, then you are truly disciples of Mine.

John 15:7, 9-10 – If you abide in Me, and My words abide in you, ask whatever you wish, and it shall be done for you . . . . Just as the Father has loved Me, I have also loved you; abide in My love. If you keep My commandments, you will abide in My love; just as I have kept My Father's commandments, and abide in His love.

1 Peter 1:23 – For you have been born again not of seed which is perishable but imperishable, that is, through the living and abiding word of God.

1 John 2:10 – The one who loves his brother abides in the light and there is no cause for stumbling in him.

1 John 2:14 – ... because you are strong, and the word of God abides in you, and you have overcome the evil one.

1 John 2:24 – As for you, let that abide in you which you heard from the beginning. If what you heard from the beginning abides in you, you also will abide in the Son and in the Father.

1 John 4:16 – God is love, and the one who abides in love abides in God, and God abides in him.

2 John 1:2 – ... for the sake of the truth which abides in us and will be with us forever.

2 John 1:9 – Anyone who goes too far and does not abide in the teaching of Christ, does not have God; the one who abides in the teaching, he has both the Father and the Son.

Being Totally Committed to God/the Lord

2 Chronicles 16:9 – For the eyes of the Lord move to and fro throughout the earth that He may strongly support those whose heart is completely His .....

Luke 9:23 – If anyone wishes to come after Me, let him deny himself, and take up his cross daily, and follow Me.

Further Reading

A' Kempis, Thomas. *The Imitation of Christ.* Ed. Paul M. Bechtel. Chicago: Moody Press, 1980. There are many worthwhile editions of this book.

Balswick, Judith and Boni Piper. *Life Ties: Cultivating Relationships that Make Life Worth Living.* Downers Grove: InterVarsity Press, 1995.

Bonhoeffer, Dietrich. *The Cost of Discipleship.* London: SCM Press Ltd., 1959; reprinted New York: Touchstone Books, Simon & Schuster Inc., 1995.

Bridges, Jerry. *The Practice of Godliness.* Colorado Springs: NavPress, 1988.

Carney, Glandion and William Long. *Longing for God: Prayer and the Rhythms of Life.* Downers Grove: InterVarsity Press, 1993.

Crabb, Larry. *Finding God.* Grand Rapids: Zondervan Publishing House, 1993.

_____. *Inside Out.* Colorado Springs: NavPress, 1988.

Edwards, Tilden. *Living in the Presence: Spiritual Exercises to Open Our Lives to the Awareness of God.* San Francisco: HarperCollins Publishers, 1995

Eyre, Stephen D. *Drawing Close to God: The Essentials of a Dynamic Quiet Time.* A Lifeguide Resource. Downers Grove: InterVarsity Press, 1995.

_____. *Entering God's Presence: A Month of Guided Quiet Times. Spiritual Encounter Guides.* Downers Grove: InterVarsity Press, 1992.

_____ and Jacalyn Eyre. *Abiding in Christ's Love: A Month of Guided Quiet Times in John 13-17. Spiritual Encounter Guides.* Downers Grove: InterVarsity Press, 1994.

Guyon, Jeanne. *Experiencing the Depths of Jesus Christ.* Gardiner, ME: Christian Books, n.d.

Hession, Roy and Revel Hession. *We Would See Jesus.* Fort Washington, PA: Christian Literature Crusade, 1958.

Hettinga, Jan David. *Follow Me: Experience the Loving Leadership of Jesus.* Colorado Springs: NavPress, 1996.

Holmes, Arthur F. *All Truth Is God's Truth.* Downers Grove: InterVarsity Press, 1977.

Hybels, Bill. *Who You Are (When No One's Looking): Choosing Consistency, Resisting Compromise.* Downers Grove: InterVarsity Press, 1987.

Lawrence, Brother. *The Practice of the Presence of God.* Trans. John J. Delaney. New York: Image Books, published by Doubleday, 1977.

Longenecker, Richard N., Editor. *Patterns of Discipleship in the New Testament.* Grand Rapids: William B. Eerdmans Publishing Company, 1996. This is a fairly academic book.

McDermott, Gerald R. *Seeing God: Twelve Reliable Signs of True Spirituality.* Downers Grove: InterVarsity Press, 1995.

McGrath, Alister. *Spirituality in an Age of Change: Rediscovering the Spirit of the Reformers.* Grand Rapids: Zondervan Publishing House, 1994.

Metzger, Will. *Tell the Truth: The Whole Gospel to the Whole Person by Whole People – A Training Manual on the Message and Methods of God-Centered Witnessing.* Second Edition. Downers Grove: InterVarsity, 1984.

Mulholland, M. Robert Jr. *Invitation to a Journey: A Road Map for Spiritual Formation.* Downers Grove: InterVarsity Press, 1993.

Ortlund, Ray and Anne. *In His Presence.* Eugene, OR: Harvest House Publishers, 1995.

Packer, J.I. *Knowing God.* Downers Grove: InterVarsity Press, 1973.

Peterson, Eugene H. *A Long Obedience in the Same Direction: Discipleship in an Instant Society.* Downers Grove: InterVarsity Press, 1980.

_____. Take and Read – *Spiritual Reading: An Annotated List.* Grand Rapids: William B. Eerdmans Publishing Company, 1996.

Phillips, Michael. *A God to Call Father: Discovering Intimacy with God.* Wheaton: Tyndale House Publishers, 1995.

Piper, John. *Desiring God: Meditations of a Christian Hedonist.* Portland, OR: Multnomah Books, 1985.

Rogers, Adrian. *The Power of His Presence.* Wheaton: Crossway Books, 1995.

Sanders, J. Oswald. *Enjoying Intimacy with God.* Chicago: Moody Press, 1980.

Smith, Chuck. *Why Grace Changes Everything.* Eugene, OR: Harvest House Publishers, 1994.

Sproul, R.C. *The Soul's Quest for God.* Wheaton: Tyndale House Publishers, 1992.

Stafford, Tim. *Knowing the Face of God: Deepening Your Personal Relationship with God.* Revised ed. Grand Rapids: Zondervan Publishing House, 1989.

Stanford, Miles J. *Principles of Spiritual Growth.* Lincoln, NE: Back to the Bible Publications, 1976.

Stokes, Penelope J. *Faith: The Substance of Things Unseen – Discovering Deeper Faith and True Intimacy with God.* Wheaton: Tyndale House Publishers, 1995.

Stott, John R.W. *Basic Christianity,* Second Edition. Downers Grove: InterVarsity Press, 1971.

Tozer, A.W. *The Pursuit of God.* Harrisburg, PA: Christian Publications, Inc., 1948.

Wilkes, Peter. *Winning the War Within: How to Stop Doing What You Don't Want to Do.* Downers Grove: InterVarsity Press, 1995.

Yancey, Philip. *Finding God in Unexpected Places.* Nashville: Moorings, a division of the Ballantine Publishing Group, Random House, Inc., 1995.

_____. *The Jesus I Never Knew.* Grand Rapids: Zondervan Publishing House, 1995.

About the Author

Michael F. Sabo has been serving on staff with The Navigators since 1980. He ministers among Christian Leaders and the Unchurched in Colorado and throughout the United States. In addition, Michael serves as a Transitional pastor within Colorado churches.

Michael is founder and president of Christian Leadership Institute (CLI). CLI is an alternative to traditional seminary training utilizing seven different venues of training. For further details please see our website: www.ChristianLeadershipInst.org

Michael earned his Ph.D. at Trinity International University (TIU), located in Deerfield, Illinois. Since 1985 he has been an adjunct faculty member at TIU and since 2002 Michael has served as adjunct faculty at Denver Seminary. His courses focus on *Personal Holiness, Lifestyle Evangelism, Discipleship, Spiritual Formation, Leader Development, Developing a Ministry Philosophy* and *Critical Thinking Skills and the Art of Asking Questions.* Michael and his wife, Darlene, reside in Colorado Springs, CO and have four adult children.

Copies of this book may be ordered from www.Amazon.com.

Made in the USA
Charleston, SC
21 February 2013